The Witches' Almanac

Spring 2011 —

CONTAINING pictorial and explicit delineations of the
magical phases of the Moon together with information about astrological
portents of the year to come and various aspects of occult knowledge
enabling all who read to improve their lives in the old manner.

The Witches' Almanac, Ltd.

Publishers   Providence, Rhode Island
www.TheWitchesAlmanac.com

Address all inquiries and information to
THE WITCHES' ALMANAC, LTD.
P.O. Box 1292
Newport, RI   02840-9998

10-ISBN: 0-9824323-0-5
13-ISBN: 978-0-9824323-0-3

ISSN: 1522-3183

First Printing August 2010

Printed in Canada

Printed on 100% recycled paper

Established 1971 by Elizabeth Pepper

Preface

THIS YEAR THE ALMANAC is dedicated to Stones and the Powers of Earth.

Stones represent the foundation of our existence. They correspond to the element of earth – symbolizing security, protection, strength and support. Of course, with these powers comes the risk of their loss.

With the solstice of 2011 upon us, this year of stones will be a challenging one. As wise practitioners, we choose to use our skills to brave this obstacle. Our ability will be confronted by upcoming changes in life around us and in the world at large. We must remember that when challenges are presented, they are almost always accompanied by opportunities. The clever will brave the challenge and embrace the opportunity. This year will be a time to have the powers of stones and earth settle in our spiritual being and form a place of balance, a centering point for us to gain personal strength. By finding our personal center, we bring equilibrium to mankind.

Once again, we have chosen a series of articles to bring you closer to the heartbeat of the witch – one who works with our natural surroundings and has a keen eye and a sensitive ear to recognize the subtle changes in the life of our planet.

Our readers and our staff have lost a true friend when our editor, Barbara Stacy, passed out of this world in 2010. In this issue we have presented you with several articles by our beloved Barbara. Her writing skills and quick wit will be deeply missed.

The Witches' Almanac is ever searching for ways to bring you, the reader, a better understanding of the old ways of traditional witchcraft. Visit our website (www.TheWitchesAlmanac. com) and browse our "What's new at *The Witches' Almanac*," found in the back of this issue.

In Memoriam

An age has passed... but a tradition continues

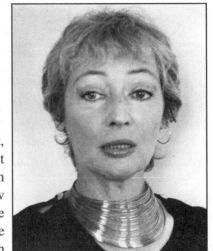

AS fate would have it, two young, intelligent and spunky women crossed paths in New York City in the late 1940's. They were none other than Elizabeth Pepper and Barbara Stacy. Elizabeth was the art director at *Gourmet Magazine* and Barbara was writing and editing magazines for Ideal Publishing. Soon thereafter, Barbara also joined the staff at *Gourmet* and a friendship that would last a lifetime was formed – reaching into the 21st century and halted on this plane only by death. Elizabeth passed in July of 2005 to be joined by Barbara on May 5th of 2010.

Barbara Stacy, charming, intelligent and gifted with wit sharper than a razor's edge, had an indomitable spirit. Born in New Haven, CT in 1926, she briefly attended the University of Connecticut and the Yale School of Drama, and in Barbara's own words, "hastily achieved dropout status in both." Nothing less than the Big Apple could satisfy Barbara's thirst for life and craving for adventure. She spent the fifties on the editorial staff at *Gourmet Magazine* and then took a copy writing position for a public relations firm. *The Witches' Almanac* made its debut in 1971 – Barbara's myriad contributions as a writer and editor enlivening its pages from its earliest days. In 1980 Barbara accepted a position as copy editor with the *PacificSun* and moved to Marin County, California. She finally moved to North Miami Beach, Florida with her husband, musician Eddie Caine.

By the time Barbara "retired" to Florida, she had already authored *The Alitalia Book of Authentic Italian Cookery*, *Ancient Roman Holidays*, and the original *Magical Creatures* with co-author Elizabeth Pepper. If anything, the two became closer in their later years; their joint venture, *The Witches' Almanac*, providing endless fodder for debate and countless reasons to keep in touch on a regular basis. When Elizabeth passed, Barbara made a choice each and every day to keep the legacy alive. Few readers know that Barbara was struck by illness in her twilight years, bedridden most of the day for close to a decade. Yet she never faltered in her responsibilities as an associate editor and even researched and authored an entire new work single-handedly – her last published book titled *Greek Gods in Love.*

Barbara could edit an entire paragraph – over the phone – in less than a minute; deleting nothing more than the 17 characters that just couldn't be squeezed onto the page and leaving the meaning intact. She took great pride in her research for each and every piece she wrote. Barbara delighted in humor and found it around every corner. She was endlessly fascinated by ancient myths, traditional stories and literature of every shape and size. Language was her playground, and Barbara Stacy was always "king of the hill."

We will miss her contributions as our esteemed Associate Editor, but most of all we will miss Barbara and the unexpected turn of phrase that was part of every conversation, certain to evoke a lingering smile or a full-fledged belly laugh that had to be shared with another member of the staff as soon as possible. We know that she missed Elizabeth dearly and we are convinced that they are reunited, watching over the legacy that is The Witches' Almanac, Ltd. Our lives are enriched for having known these two amazing women and we dare to believe that they have reached beyond the pages of our publications to enrich your lives as well. Indeed, an age has passed... but we will continue the tradition by striving for authenticity, integrity and quality in all of our future publications.

Brief Encounter with a Higher Power

AT AGE TEN I corner my mother in the kitchen to tell her that I do not believe in God. She yells that if I talk like that, God will strike me dead. I walk into the dining room where there is a rug, thump to the floor, and remain immobile. My mother comes running and lets out a scream, real fright. Now I get scared, not of the wrath of a God I don't believe in but of the wrath of my mother, which I have good reason to believe in. I am too frightened to move, because as soon as I get up I know I am in for it. And the longer I lay there the more hysterical my mother grows. Finally I stand up and she gives me one hell of a smack on the tush. It does not renew my faith in the Almighty, but it does renew a healthy respect for a higher power.

– BARBARA STACY
from Brief Encounters

❦ HOLIDAYS ❦

Spring 2011 to Spring 2012

Art Director . . . . Karen Marks

Astrologer . . . . Dikki-Jo Mullen

Climatologist . . . . Tom C. Lang

Cover Art and Design. . . Ogmios MacMerlin

Production Consultant . . . . Robin Antoni

Sales . . . . Ellen Lynch

Shipping, Bookkeeping . . . . D. Bullock

ANDREW THEITIC
Executive Editor

BARBARA STACY
JEAN MARIE WALSH
Associate Editors

JUDIKA ILLES
Copy Editor

CONTENTS

Thrice Toss These Oaken Ashes

Thrice toss these oaken ashes in the air,
Thrice sit thou mute in this enchanted chair,
Then thrice three times tie up this true
   love's knot,
And murmur soft "She will, or she will not."

Go burn these poisonous weeds in
   yon blue fire,
These screech owl's feathers and this
   prickling briar,
This cypress gathered at a dead man's grave,
That all my fears and cares an end may have.

Then come, you fairies! dance with me
   a round;
Melt her hard heart with your melodious
   sound.
In vain are all the charms I can devise:
She hath an art to break them with her eyes.

– THOMAS CAMPION, 1567-1620

Yesterday, Today and Tomorrow

by Barbara Stacy

SWANS OF CORNISH WITCHES. The ancient region of Cornwall, England, has a long history of odd sacred rituals. Among them, an  archaeological bonanza some years ago unearthed 30 small pits (15 inches by 6 inches) lined with swan's feathers. The little earthly nests also included dead magpies, emblematic of the region, as well as eggs, quartz pebbles, nail clippings and a chunk of iron cauldron. The discovery, dating from the seventeenth century, added plenty to the mystery quotient. According to Jacqui Wood, leader of the excavation, "Killing a swan at this time would have been incredibly risky, because they were the property of the Crown." The period also marked turmoil in England, when Puritans devoted themselves to destroying any links to paganism, and witchcraft

called for a death sentence. Wood speculates that perhaps swan feathers had a connection with fertility and reflected secret offerings. We have no clue, written or anecdotal, depicting the unique rituals enacted with the lovely birds. They still glide around Cornwall in all their elegance, white as the surf that laces the shores.

ARRIVEDERCI, VAMPIRE. Apparently sixteenth-century Venetians knew how to deal with vampires. An archaeological dig has unearthed the remains of a woman's jaw held agape with a brick. Experts believe that the bizarre burial indicates an ancient ritual for persuading vampires to cease and desist their thirsty ways with the living. The skeleton lay in a mass grave created during a plague epidemic. Its brick restraint is unique. "Vampires don't exist," declares archaeologist/anthropologist Matteo Borrini, who nevertheless rejoices in the importance of the discovery: "For the first time we have found evidence of an exorcism against a vampire."

DIM VIEW OF ROBBIN' HOOD. In our time we feel affection for the romantic figure of Robin Hood. We picture him a mythological superstar, gorgeous in green from head to toe, lord of Sherwood Forest, arrows at the ready to rob the rich and give to the poor. It comes as some surprise that Robin may not have been so highly regarded by earlier standards. John Luxford, a Scottish art historian, recently discovered a note in the margin of a thirteenth-century Latin manuscript. The comment, scribbled in ink a century later by a medieval monk: "Around this time, according to popular opinion, a certain outlaw named Robin Hood, with his accomplices, infested Sherwood and other law-abiding areas of England with continuous robberies." *Infested?* Should we rethink the Robin Hood myth?

BEES LOVE PARIS TOO. Alarmed at the dwindling number of bees in the countryside, the French have set up hives atop some famous Paris rooftops. Everyone loves the parks and gardens of the City of Lights, bees no exception. They have made themselves right at home, sweetly thanking host beekeepers with terrific amounts of honey.

The new hives have been established atop the Grand Palais Exhibition Hall, the Opera Bastille and the Palais Garnier, among others. The Luxembourg Gardens bees buzz around in peaceful coexistence with *marionnette* enthusiasts and kids sailing model boats. Rural bees have been slowing down on the job, producing 20 to 40 pounds of

honey per harvest. Their more vital city cousins yield about 110 to 130 pounds per harvest, sold to the public in September to fund more hives. Pesticides are one of the primary reasons for country bees taking such a heavy hit. In Paris, pesticides are a *non non* in all parks and gardens. Bees respond by doing what bees do best – their magic act, transforming nectar into honey.

A BRIDGE TOO SPOOKY. Like crossroads, stairways and doorways, bridges seem to attract tales of haunting. Pleasant Hill Road Bridge in Etowah County, Alabama, has its own ghost story and proceeds into another chapter. The structure, too expensive to maintain, has been cut in half for moving to another site. One part already has moved to a trial site. Locals wait with apprehension to determine if oddities will continue in either half or cease altogether. "I didn't feel comfortable driving on it, and it was haunted on top of that," said one woman. People declared that crossing the "crybaby bridge" evoked voices. Parking on the structure also drew feelings of malaise – foreboding that if the car shifted into neutral, haunting spirits would push it over to the other side. Some bridges inspiring fear are associated with tragedies, but no historical records yield such a clue to Pleasant Hill Road. So far, no word from either of the split sites.

FILIPINO "DRESSING THE DEAD." A few members of the Hanunuo Mang-yan tribe of Mindoro still celebrate an ancient tradition of reviving the dead. The *kulcot*, which means "scratch" or "unearth," consists of clothing the corpse in a ritual form. A year after burial, the family gathers and exhumes the remains. The skeleton is cleaned, the parts wrapped in a large cloth and ceremonially tied and draped in such a bulky way as to resemble the human figure. Few Mangyans have mastered the skill of creating the correct mannequin image, the *sinakot*. Each son and daughter contributes clothes and jewelry, and the mummified revival is greeted in the village with gongs and dances. The family keeps the *sinakot* in a hut for a year and then transfers the figure to a cave where others are housed. Dressing the dead ceremonies, like other traditions, have largely vanished as villagers from coastal areas flock to cities for jobs. According to one rueful Mangyan, "The younger members of the tribe are not interested in performing this ancient ritual of ours. They don't know how to do it."

PARK YOUR CARCASS. Are all big-city dwellers starting to go nuts for some green space? A few years ago activists established Parking Day in San Francisco, now celebrated by over a hundred cities around the world. Each greenie seized a parking space at curbside and set up a mini-park. Some went for sod and arranged potted plants and lawn chairs for relaxation, perhaps browsing through "Walden Pond" for inspiration. Others went beachy with sand or featured kiddie pools. One neighborhood association in Los Angeles captured seven parking spaces

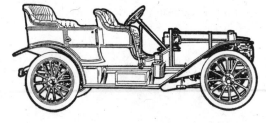

and offered a hangout with a barbecue grill and workshop about drought-resistant plants. In Chicago, two spaces were transformed into a pit stop for bicyclists to chill out and refuel on drinks and munchies. The idea is to encourage awareness of traffic congestion and pollution, pointing out the delights of grass over asphalt. It's fun street theater, of course, perhaps appreciated least by drivers circling and circling blocks as if seeking parking in earthly hell.

ROCK ON. Travelling stones are as

rare as travelling trees, but a phenomenon in Death Valley confounds geologists as much as tourists. The site offering the mineral mysteries is Racetrack Playa, a shoreline track along a seven-mile seasonally dry lake in Inyo County, California. The playa is dotted with "sailing stones" that leave straight, curved or zigzag trails. There they pop up, from boulders to small rocks, their travel routes noted but movements never witnessed. Freaky curiosity, two prevailing theories: Once the lake is flooded, enough clay is created to allow winter winds up to 90 miles an hour to launch stones along the slippery way. Second possibility; ice forms at night when the temperature falls below freezing on the lake, wind drives the heavy ice cubes onto the playa. When the ice melts, the stones are where the stones are. Maybe the movements, long famous, never witnessed, work either or neither way – your guess is as good as ours.

Dana

Goddess of the Fey

THE Tuatha Dé Danann are an ancient race of people in Irish mythology, the fifth race to colonize and conquer the Emerald Isle. Their name, which means "Children of Dana," pays tribute to a primordial goddess. The Tuatha Dé Danann, Dana's Children, were eventually conquered by the Gaels, the present Irish people. In response, they retreated underground, inhabiting barrows, mounds and hills. The Tuatha Dé Danann transformed into the Sidhe (pronounced *shee*), the Irish name for the fairy folk or the fey. As befitting these powerful spirits, their ancestress Dana is a grand and powerful goddess.

Dana (pronounced *Dawn-uh* or *Day-na*) is the ancient Celtic goddess of the fairies. Throughout the Celtic world, she is the special friend and caretaker of the fey. Sometimes called Danu (*Dawn-oo*), this deity is also equated with the Welsh mother goddess Don. Her name may be the inspiration for the great Danube River, a region once inhabited by Celts.

Dana is associated with handicrafts, fire keeping, and manifestation ritual magic. A tremendous source of inspiration, she can be invoked for general creativity as well as for fertility. Dana is a High Priestess who shares and transmits profound spiritual teachings. Dana is a goddess of alchemy, revealing secrets of transmutation – perhaps she is responsible for the Tuatha Dé Danann's transformation into fairies.

Dana's tarot card is The Empress. Amber and all stones with natural holes are her talismans. A perfect summary of her archetypal attributes is suggested by the Old Irish root word "*dan,*" which translates as "knowledge." In Sanskrit and Pali, which are Indo-European languages as are the Celtic tongues, Dana means "generosity" and "giving" whereas among the Scandinavian *vitki* and rune casters, Dana means "woman of Denmark."

– ELAINE NEUMEIER

13

Divine White Mare

In stables, garlands of roses

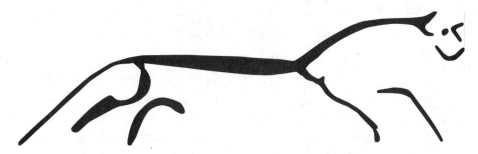

A FEW MILES south of Uffington, incised into the chalk bedrock of the hilly English countryside, stretches the gigantic figure of a horse at full gallop. Angular and abstract, elegant and mysterious, the white form measures 374 feet from muzzle to tail. Experts believe it dates from the late Bronze Age, about 1000 BCE, and may be a tribute to Epona, the ancient Celtic horse goddess. Now largely shrouded by time, the "Divine White Mare" had epochs of glory.

Epona worship arose in Gaul, flourished with the conquering Romans and traveled with the legions throughout Britain. The goddess was especially worshipped by the cavalry and turned up everywhere in Roman stables and barracks. Somewhere in the rafters an icon of Epona and her horses would turn up, sometimes depicted with foals on her lap. She often holds a basket of corn or fruit, especially apples. Sometimes Epona is riding, always "lady style," never astride. She may be lying back along the horse but never sidesaddle – the goddess sits the horse on the side

as if on a chair, legs dangling over the animal's flanks.

The deity loved roses, and soldiers believed that decked with garlands of the fragrant flower she worked protective magic. Tiny clay images of Epona were available for travel, tucked into tunics or saddle trappings for luck in battle.

Charioteers were the athletes of the military, and they too relied on Epona to keep them safe in the perilous sport. Eight annual Equirra celebrations in holiday-mad Rome honored horses, the chief festivity dedicated to Epona on December 18. The daredevils drove two- or four-horse chariots around a tight oval in the Circus Maximus, cheered on by over two thousand bloodthirsty spectators. It

took immense skill not to be hurled out on the turns; an official on the sidelines threw water on the smoking wheels. For the victor, a laurel wreath, palm and glory. For Epona, adoration.

On horseback or off, mother for all

Other than as battle goddess, the White Mare has profound dominions especially appealing to women. Epona also personifies an early fertility goddess, a protective deity, in icons offering the symbolic horn of plenty. Sometimes Epona is depicted as a goddess of rivers and thermal springs, a naked water nymph in such shrines. When an Epona image holds a key, she is honored as a psychopomp – guide to the underworld land of the dead. As a crossroads symbol, the goddess is conceived as an intermediary between the living and the dead or between day and night. And especially in Ireland she has a connection with nightmares. Beyond the horse, she is especially protective of oxen, cattle and donkeys, a lover of dogs and birds.

Some viewers perceive the Uffington figure as a dragon rather than a horse, perhaps the site of the battle with St. George. Who knows? It is difficult to reconstruct the mind set of Iron Age people and the purpose of such quirky vestiges. But we do know the prodigious figure has inspired awe down the ages. Since ancient times, every seven years the local lord hosted a three-day festival at the spot, fun and games, including wrestling and cheese rolling down the hillsides – how Merrie England is that? The basic purpose of the event was to clean up overgrowth and scour the horse to the whiteness of new blizzard. The celebrations lapsed about a hundred years ago, but the English Heritage is responsible for the site and keeps things nicely pristine, thank you.

– BARBARA STACY

CELESTIAL POWERS

Lightning gods, bolts from the blue

FROM ANCIENT TIMES and ancient places, the supreme deity controlled the sky. People tended to call them thunder gods rather than lightning gods, but thunder is only bluster. Lightning is the boss and its power manifests in formidable numbers. A bolt can travel at the speed of 130,000 mph and reach a temperature of 54,000 degrees F. In its area lightning immediately sizzles the air to 36,000 degrees F., about three times hotter than the surface of the sun. This sudden intensity constricts the clear air, producing a supersonic shock wave sliding acoustically into the boom of thunder that sends pets and sometimes people hiding under beds.

Since sound fails to lend itself to image, "thunder gods" are depicted with lightning bolts. The zigzag icon serves as the main attribute of Zeus, for instance, along with the eagle and the scepter. In 265 BCE Theocritus writes of the Greek deity, "Sometimes Zeus is clear, sometimes he rains." The name of Zeus, supreme ruler of Mount Olympus, derives from *dios*, "bright," and he is also known as Zeus Astrapios, "lightbringer."

The Romans know a wondrous pantheon when they find it. When Zeus emerges as Jupiter, the newborn sky god assumes the same attributes – Jupiter too has a bolt to hurl, an eagle, a scepter and even more weather nomenclature. Known as Dios Pater, Shining Father, he is also worshipped as Jupiter Elicius (weather, storms), Jupiter Fulgurator (lightning), Jupiter Lucetius (lightning), Jupiter Pluvius (rain).

Thor, the Norse weather deity, has his own lightning icon made by dwarves – the hammer Mjollnir, "that smashes." When Thor throws the hammer,

lightning flashes. Then Mjollnir returns like a boomerang to his right hand, on which Thor wears an iron glove. Sometimes the red-bearded giant blasts lightning bolts from the eyes, adding to his ferocious appearance. The Norse believe that Thor creates thunder when he rumbles through the sky on a carriage pulled by two goats, Tanngrisni (Gap Tooth) and Tanngnost (Tooth Grinder).

Our early fore-fathers believe that the most powerful of gods control the weather, weather controls fertility and fertility controls survival.

Power cult, lesser known

Perkons prevails as a pagan weather god less known to us, but widely venerated throughout the old Baltic pantheon. In Latvia, Lithuania, Prussia, and sometimes Russia, the deity turns up in powerful fertil-ity rites as agri-culture begins to put down roots. The cult contin-ues until twelfth-century restrictions, sometimes underground, and pock-ets of practice may still be found in the region. A Catholic clergyman, D. Fabricius, writes in 1610: "During a drought, when there has not been rain, they worship Perkons in thick forests on hills and sacrifice to him a black calf, a black goat and a black cock. When the animals are killed, then, accord-ing to their custom, the people come together from all the vicin-ity, to eat and drink there together. They pay homage to Perkons by first pouring him beer, which is first brought around the fire, and at last pour it in this fire, asking Perkons to give them rain."

The god's whole family helps with his work, resonat-ing farming tradi-tion skyward. The sons strike light-ning and thunder, the mother and daughters send rain, and the daughter-in-law peals thunder to rival the deity's own ear-cracking level. The Perkons cult appeals to him in folk songs. One peasant sings to bring rain because "the shoots of barley are faded;" another lyric gives thanks for the autumn harvest.

The Heavenly Wedding

Beyond the rustic, Perkons offers more complexity. He is also depicted bris-tling with weapons, a "silver rider on a golden horse," the answer to an old riddle. He bears a sword, an iron rod, a golden whip, a fiery club, a gun, a knife. Among the arms he always car-ries is a "thunder ball," which helps to create lightning, thunder and mastery of the Devil. Many of the god's fol-lowers wear small axes on their cloth-ing as adornments. The axe amulets represent thunder

balls – symbols of symbols – believed to heal illnesses.

Legends abound, sometimes centering on food. Perkons drowns Baba because she has violated a ritual by giving him spoiled food. In another story a foe holds out bread and butter, concealing a knife in the other hand. Folk belief has it that setting out food for the god calms storms and that honeycombs thrown into a fire dispels clouds.

In the Heavenly Wedding tale, Perkons rides off to bless an event of mythological splendor – the marriage of the Moon, Menulis, to Saule, daughter of the Sun. On his way Perkons stops to strike an oak tree, his own attribute; the twisted roots are a favorite hiding place of the Devil. In Latvian folklore especially, the evil spirit is depicted as stupid, taunting, easily tricked and Perkons' prime adversary. Once his tree is rid of the evil spirit, the fertility god proceeds to the wedding and sanctifies bride and bridegroom.

As for the marriage, however blessed, an old Latvian ballad shuns any "happily ever after" whipped cream on the wedding cake:

In the first blush of Spring
  Saule and Menulis married.
Saule rose early, leaving
  Menulis's side.

Menulis went out on his own.
Menulis made love to Ausrine.
Perku-nas, with great anger,
Struck Menulis with his sword.
"Why did you leave Saule?
Why did you make love to Ausrine?
Why did you wander about
  in the dark?"

The song explains why the Sun shines during the day and the Moon shines at night, according to fabled belief – he there, she here, she there, he here. Although apart, they both desire to sojourn below and share beloved Daughter Earth.

– BARBARA STACY

And when you want the Love of anyone write on clean Parchment and that as well as ye can with all you Skill.

> *Elves whom no one sees*
> *Under the roots of Trees*
> *Deep in the antient Hills*
> *I pray of your good Wils*
> *By the white bear's paw,*
> *And the grey wolf's jaw,*
> *The Serpent's back,*
> *And Foxes track,*
> *Give me the Stone*
> *Whose power is known*
> *Unto you alone!*

Then you will find a Stone in the cup, be it a Peble or a Gemm. And if ye touch a Man or Woman on the Brows with it you will get their Love. But this is not lightly come by for they give not this stone to everybody.

– A sneak preview from
The Witchcraft of Dame Darrel of York
coming December 2010

Cauldrons

Stirring up Celtic magic

TO THE ancient Celts the iron vessel over a fire was a familiar sight, but their vivacious imagination soared with the everyday image. The cauldron turns up repeatedly in the medieval Mabinogion tales with a wide range of significance. In various contexts the icon represents the divine womb from which all life springs; the source of endless sustenance; the preserver of spooky potions; the container of odd effects; the receptacle of divine inspiration for poets; a portal to the Abyss. Water or watery creatures often connect with cauldron myths.

Zombie maker

King Bran, gigantic son of the sea god Llyr, possesses a cauldron of singular talents. Bran the Blessed, also known as the Raven, is semi-human, crowned a king of Britain. His cauldron can revive the slain, if only to a mute zombie state – but deadly effective for battle.

The cauldron features in a lethal fight within Bran's own clan. His sister Branwen is courted by Matholwch, King of Ireland, who gives Bran horses to win favor. Their half-brother Efnisien arrives at the wedding feast, outraged that he has not been consulted. He retaliates by mutilating the horses. The royal bridegroom is so furious that Bran propitiates him with the magical cauldron.

As time passes Branwen is cruelly treated by her husband. Bran sails to Ireland with an army to rescue his sister, but the Irish have the advantage. With the magic cauldron, dead warriors return to life and fight on in eerie silence. To deter the renewable army, Efnisien throws himself into the cauldron to break it. He succeeds and destroys the magic, but his heart bursts

with the effort. Bran also dies, his head severed and buried in England. Legend has it that as long as Bran's head remains in England, the realm lives on.

Wisdom maker

The sorceress Cerridwen also possesses marvelous magic, the Cauldron of Wisdom and Inspiration. She is the grieving mother of a hideous son, but determined to make him into the world's greatest bard. With the help of the cauldron, he would sing so gloriously that people would overlook his ugliness.

To kindle the cauldron's power requires gathering and seething plants for a year and a day under constant vigilance. Into the pot daily Cerridwen casts the peculiar greenery, whispering incantations. She has captured a boy named Gwion and set him to the task of stirring the cauldron whenever she has business elsewhere. At the completion of the mandated time, the cauldron itself utters a cry, produces three drops of divine wisdom and shatters. The burning drops splash Gwion's hand and with a cry the boy puts his fingers into his mouth, consuming the spell that Cerridwen has intended for her son. The wisdom of all time and poetic inspiration descends on him. Gwion transforms into Taliesin, greatest of the Welsh bards.

Trick maker

Lleu Llaw Gyffes appears in the tales as a Divine Warrior, "the lion with a steady hand."

He is under a curse that prevents him from marrying a mortal woman. But the royal magician creates lovely Blodeuwedd, a bride fashioned from flowers. The couple lives happily, adored by all the realm, until Blodeuwedd falls in love.

The "Aspect of Flowers" becomes lovers with the hunter Gronw and conspires to kill her husband. But Lleu is under another magical spell, this one protective. He can only be slain if he has one foot in a tub of water (the divine female image) and one foot on a goat (the horned male image). Blodeuwedd laughingly persuades him to enact the ludicrous position. Lleu humors his wife and suspends himself in the air between the elements. Hidden nearby, Gronw springs out and pierces him with a spear. Lleu cries out in agony, takes the form of an eagle and flies into an oak tree. He is rescued and restored by his sorcerer uncle, Gwydion. Together they wreak revenge on the evildoers. Lleu kills Gronw with a spear. Blodeuwedd is turned into an owl, doomed to dwell alone in darkness, shunned by other birds.

– RHIANNON McBRIDE

Tulip Mania

Flowers inspire a bizarre bull market

IN 1624, a rich Dutch merchant was offered three thousand guilders for one of only two existing Semper Augustus tulip bulbs. He turned down the offer, hoping for more. The sum reflected a lavish annual income of golden coins or about twice what Rembrandt received for "The Night Watch." How could one flower command such a fortune?

The fact is, the whole populace had gone gaga over tulips. First imported from Constantinople, they were a rarity, an expensive status symbol. Other cultures adored the orchid for its erotic beauty or the rose for its ruffled skirt and fragrance. But the elegant tulip, its glorious colors shimmering in the gray climate, went to Dutch hearts in a big way. The flower was the glory of the elaborate gardens that surrounded mansions along the canals.

About this time a horticultural fluke added an even more spectacular quality to the silky petals. The tulips contracted mosaic, a rather harmless virus that streaked flowers with other colors, creating the first exquisite flame patterns. Nature seemed to be redesigning its own perfection. Now Dutch businessmen controlled a unique product with value that exploded from expensive to through the roof, both at home and in international trade.

Get-rich-quick fever

Prices rose steadily throughout the 1630s. For investors, flowers are more pleasurable to collect than stocks and bonds – although tulips themselves became, in effect, stocks and bonds, trading briskly on the Dutch stock market. That fortunes were being created did not go unobserved; speculators slipped their way into the market. Tulip investments became the delusional "sure thing" that occasionally shakes up a whole country. People mortgaged or traded in their farms, homes, land, livestock and life savings, sometimes to acquire a single bulb. These buyers had no intention of planting tulips – the bulbs were simply chips for trading up. Haarlem, the chief business center, was suffering from the bubonic plague during the period, a circumstance which also may have favored fatalistic risk taking.

For some, the returns were dizzying. By 1636 any bulb, including those once considered garbage fodder, could fetch hundreds of guilders. In less than one month, the price of tulip bulbs went up twentyfold. One period receipt lists the merchandise a farmer paid for one prized Viceroy bulb: "2 lasts of wheat, 2 lasts of rye, 4 fat oxen, 8 fat swine, 12 fat sheep, 2 hogsheads wine, 4 tuns beer, 2 tuns butter, 1,000 pounds cheese, 1 suit clothes, 1 bed complete, 1 silver cup." The total – worth 2,500 guilders or florins.

The flowers were bought and sold in taverns all over Holland, always a hot ticket, no sooner bought than sold, sometimes flipping as much as ten times a day. The mania reached its peak in the winter of 1636/1637. An auction arose

to benefit seven orphans whose only assets were seventy fine tulips left by their father. The best was a rare Violetten Admirael van Enkhuizen, the bulb about to be split in half, which sold for 5,200 guilders. In total, the lot brought in 53,000 guilders.

Bulbs go bust

Supply began to dwindle, partly due to the leisurely horticultural character of the tulip itself. From seed to flower takes seven years of cultivation. Bulbs can produce two or three clones or "off-sets" annually; the mother bulb lasts only a few years. Tulips bloom only in April and May for about a week or two, succeeded shortly by the secondary buds. But bulbs can only be uprooted from June to September, and actual exchanges of money and product could only be conducted in those four months.

The Dutch, who established many techniques of modern finance, initiated futures contracts. If a buyer wanted to invest off season, he and the vendor signed a contract before a notary providing for an actual exchange when bulbs became available. Sometimes the process was described disparagingly as *windhandel*, wind driven – contracts with merchandise as invisible as air. Nevertheless the system worked well enough until the supply crunch and slipping prices. Contracts skidded into shortfall and the tulip trade abruptly ground to a halt, falling about 90 percent in one month.

Gamblers shocked, shocked!

Chaos prevailed nationwide. In one typical lawsuit, ten Semper Augustus bulbs had sold for the equivalent of $1,600 each, to be delivered in six weeks. Before delivery time the price of the same bulbs had tumbled, with plenty available at $120 each. The buyer refused delivery and declined to pay the $14,800 difference. Many others defaulted similarly. Howls of pain arose to government level, but the system was broken beyond repair. Traders that had invested everything in tulips were ruined, some lifetime assets a little bag of bulbs worth about as much as onions.

Down the years, no culture seems immune to occasional economic craziness – in the U.S. most recently sub-prime home mortgages; during the nineties, Silicon Valley tech-stocks; in 1929 the catastrophic stock-market crash. As for the Dutch, they still love the flower and miles of tulip gardens and nurseries gladden their hearts in spring.

Infatuation remains, but the prices have changed considerably. Eight Salvo bulbs, for instance, producing a ravishing white flower shot with crimson flames, sells for $21.99 in the Netherlands. But cast your mind back four hundred years to when tulips were simply gorgeous flowers and not the darlings of national commerce. A merchant offers to swap a few tulip bulbs for your home. Your answer would be the Dutch equivalent of are you out of your mind? In a culture of mass sanity, the response would be a no-brainer.

❋ *The Sailor and the Herring* ❋

A WEALTHY merchant had invested in a shipload of tulips from the Middle East. When the ship docked, a sailor was sent to the owner's warehouse to report on the voyage. To thank the sailor for his trouble, the merchant left the room to get a herring to give the messenger. Alone in the office on a table loaded with silks and velvets, the sailor spotted what looked like onions and filched one to go with the herring. He put the bulb in his pocket, thanked the merchant for the fish and returned to the dock.

When the trader returned, he noticed that his prized Semper Augustus, worth  3,000 florins, was missing. He raised an uproar and turned the warehouse upside down searching. Suddenly someone remembered that the sailor had been alone at the scene of the crime. The merchant and his clerks rushed down to the vessel, where they found the sailor sitting on a coil of rope and finishing his breakfast. He popped the last bite into his mouth and leaned forward to learn what all the excitement was about – and was amazed to learn that it was about him!

The sailor readily admitted that he had stolen an onion, but knew nothing about a tulip bulb. "And as a matter of fact," he complained, "it did not very much have the taste of an onion." The merchant told the astonished sailor that he had just eaten a bulb "worth more than the cost of having breakfast with the Prince of Orange and all his court." The sailor, jailed for several months, may have lost his appetite for onions, if not the salty goodness of herring.

– BARBARA STACY

If the above caused you to be tulip conscious, check out our website at http://TheWitchesAlmanac.com/Almanac Extras/. *We offer an occult connection between tulips and fairies, a garden guide for growing your own tulips, and a delightful English folk tale offering a singular use for tulip blossoms.*

The Manner of Witches

MARK YE WELL their manner, for it is quiet and assumeth not. It is in peaceful tones they speak and oft seem abstracted. Seeming to prefer the company of Beastes, they converse with them as equals. They dwell in lonely places, there better (as they say) to know the voices of the Wind and hear the secrets of Nature. Possessing the Wysdome of the fields and forests, they do harm and heal with their harvests. They concerne themselves not with idle chatter or fashion, nor do worldly goods hold worth for them. Be not confused as to think that only Woman-kynd harboureth the gifte in this matter. Of Men there bee many that hold mickle power.

– EDWARD JOHNSTON, ESQ.
Sudbury, Suffold, England 1645

MOON GARDENING

BY PHASE

Sow, transplant, bud and graft   *Plow, cultivate, weed and reap*

NEW	First Quarter	FULL	Last Quarter	NEW
Plant above-ground crops with outside seeds, flowering annuals.	Plant above-ground crops with inside seeds.	Plant root crops, bulbs, biennials, perennials.		Do not plant.

BY PLACE IN THE ZODIAC

Fruitful Signs

Cancer – Most favorable planting time for all leafy crops bearing fruit above ground. Prune to encourage growth in Cancer.

Scorpio – Second only to Cancer, a Scorpion Moon promises good germination and swift growth. In Scorpio, prune for bud development.

Pisces – Planting in the last of the Watery Triad is especially effective for root growth.

Taurus – The best time to plant root crops is when the Moon is in the sign of the Bull.

Capricorn – The Earthy Goat Moon promotes the growth of rhizomes, bulbs, roots, tubers and stalks. Prune now to strengthen branches.

Libra – Airy Libra may be the least beneficial of the Fruitful Signs, but is excellent for planting flowers and vines.

Barren Signs

Leo – Foremost of the Barren Signs, the Lion Moon is the best time to effectively destroy weeds and pests. Cultivate and till the soil.

Gemini – Harvest in the Airy Twins; gather herbs and roots. Reap when the Moon is in a sign of Air or Fire to assure best storage.

Virgo – Plow, cultivate, and control weeds and pests when the moon is in Virgo.

Sagittarius – Plow and cultivate the soil or harvest under the Archer Moon. Prune now to discourage growth.

Aquarius – This dry sign of Air is perfect for ground cultivation, reaping crops, gathering roots and herbs. It is a good time to destroy weeds and pests.

Aries – Cultivate, weed, and prune to lessen growth. Gather herbs and roots for storage.

Consult our Moon Calendar pages for phase and place in the zodiac circle. The Moon remains in a sign for about two-and-a-half days. Match your gardening activity to the day that follows the Moon's entry into that zodiac sign.

The MOON Calendar

is divided into zodiac signs rather than the more familiar Gregorian calendar.

2011

2012

Bear in mind that new projects should be initiated when the Moon is waxing (from dark to full); when the Moon is on the wane (from full to dark), it is a time for storing energy and the wise person waits.

Please note that Moons are listed by day of entry into each sign. Quarters are marked, but as rising and setting times vary from one region to another, it is advisable to check your local newspaper, library or planetarium.

The Moon's Place is computed for Eastern Standard Time.

☽ Celestial Gems ☾

METALS TO THE seven heavenly bodies of antiquity have remained constant for over two thousand years: the Sun, gold; the Moon, silver; Mars, iron; Mercury, quicksilver; Jupiter, tin; Venus, copper; and Saturn, lead. But the symbolic classification of gems is a difficult and often confusing matter, for the correspondences vary widely from one occult authority to another. By consulting a wide spectrum of sources – ancient, classical, medieval, Renaissance and modern – we've assembled a list of jewels most linked with the Sun, Moon, and some particular planets through the centuries of Western occult tradition.

Agate – *Mercury* ☿
Alexandrite – *Mercury* ☿
Amber – *Moon* ☽
Amethyst – *Jupiter* ♃
Aquamarine – *Venus* ♀
Beryl – *Venus* ♀
Bloodstone – *Mars* ♂
Carbuncle – *Venus* ♀
Carnelian – *Sun* ☉
Cat's–eye – *Sun* ☉
Chalcedony – *Saturn* ♄
Chrysoprase – *Venus* ♀
Crystal – *Moon* ☽
Diamond – *Sun* ☉
Emerald – *Venus* ♀
Garnet – *Mars* ♂
Jacinth – *Jupiter* ♃

Jade – *Venus* ♀
Jasper – *Mercury* ☿
Jet – *Saturn* ♄
Lapis lazuli – *Jupiter* ♃
Malachite – *Venus* ♀
Moonstone – *Moon* ☽
Onyx – *Saturn* ♄
Opal – *Mercury* ☿
Pearl – *Moon* ☽
Peridot – *Venus* ♀
Quartz – *Moon* ☽
Ruby – *Mars* ♂
Sapphire – *Jupiter* ♃
Sardonyx – *Mercury* ☿
Topaz – *Sun* ☉
Tourmaline – *Mercury* ☿
Turquoise – *Venus* ♀

capricorn

December 21 – January 19

Cardinal Sign of Earth ♍ Ruled by Saturn ♄

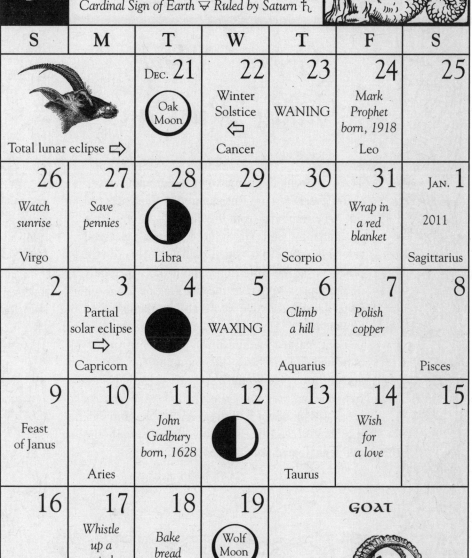

S	M	T	W	T	F	S
Total lunar eclipse ⇨		Dec. 21 Oak Moon	22 Winter Solstice ⇦ Cancer	23 WANING	24 Mark Prophet born, 1918 Leo	25
26 Watch sunrise Virgo	27 Save pennies	28 Libra	29	30 Scorpio	31 Wrap in a red blanket	Jan. 1 2011 Sagittarius
2	3 Partial solar eclipse ⇨ Capricorn	4	5 WAXING	6 Climb a hill Aquarius	7 Polish copper	8 Pisces
9 Feast of Janus	10 Aries	11 John Gadbury born, 1628	12	13 Taurus	14 Wish for a love	15
16 Gemini	17 Whistle up a wind	18 Bake bread Cancer	19 Wolf Moon	GOAT		

Northern Europeans revered the nimble goat for its playful nature. The love goddess of Germanic tribes rode a goat to May Eve revels. Thor, Norse god of thunder, drove a chariot drawn by two fierce, unruly goats.

– Magical Creatures

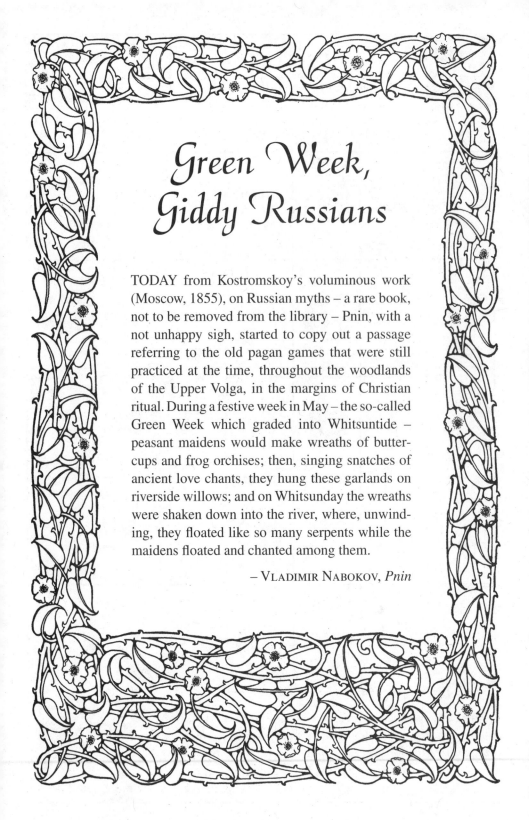

Green Week, Giddy Russians

TODAY from Kostromskoy's voluminous work (Moscow, 1855), on Russian myths – a rare book, not to be removed from the library – Pnin, with a not unhappy sigh, started to copy out a passage referring to the old pagan games that were still practiced at the time, throughout the woodlands of the Upper Volga, in the margins of Christian ritual. During a festive week in May – the so-called Green Week which graded into Whitsuntide – peasant maidens would make wreaths of buttercups and frog orchises; then, singing snatches of ancient love chants, they hung these garlands on riverside willows; and on Whitsunday the wreaths were shaken down into the river, where, unwinding, they floated like so many serpents while the maidens floated and chanted among them.

– VLADIMIR NABOKOV, *Pnin*

aquarius

January 20 – February 18

Fixed Sign of Air △ Ruled by Uranus ⛢

S	M	T	W	T	F	S
SWAN	A Native American legend of the Blackfoot tribe depicts swans as helpers in a hero's quest to visit the sun. – Magical Creatures			JAN. 20 Linda Howe born, 1942 Leo	21	22 Keep warm Virgo
23	24 Draw flowers Libra	25	26 ◑ Scorpio	27	28 Sit by the fire Sagittarius	29
30	31 Pour water from hand to earth Capricorn	FEB. 1 Oimelc Eve	2 **Year of the Rabbit** Aquarius	3 WAXING Candlemas ⇐	4 Gaze into a crystal ball Pisces	5
6 The enlightened shine	7 Charles Dickens born, 1812 Aries	8	9 Avoid stubbornness Taurus	10	11	12 ◐ Gemini
13	14 Cancer	15 Lupercalia	16 Listen to sparrows sing Leo	17	18 Storm Moon	SWAN

Apollo, Greek god of music and poetry, was linked to the bird, for it was believed that his soul passed into a swan. From this legend arose the tradition that the souls of all good poets live on as swans. Ben Jonson called Shakespeare the "Swan of Avon."
– Magical Creatures

ALDER

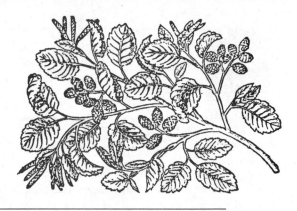

THE ALDER is usually found thriving in thickets beside lakes, streams and rivers. It so favors marshy conditions that the tree seldom grows on drier land. Its black bark scored with cracks and broad oval leaves quickly identify the alder. As the timber dries after felling, its color changes from yellow to orange to red. When dried, the wood is water resistant and does not split when nailed. For centuries alder has provided pilings to serve as building foundations throughout European lowlands. Charcoal derived from alder wood is superior to all others.

The alder is associated with Bran, a Celtic hero/god. One tale about this is found in the medieval Welsh collection of legends known as *The Mabinogian*. Another story, *The Voyage of Bran to the World Below*, occurs in Irish literature recorded in the eighth century. The sea-god Llyr (Welsh) and Lir (Irish) play a role in both tales, as do black birds: the starling, crow and raven. The Irish epic describes Bran waking from a dream to find himself in the presence of a goddess and holding in his hand a silver branch. The branch magically springs from his hand to her once he agrees to set sail for the abode of the goddess.

It is rare to find alder mentioned in European folklore. Old herbals, however, submit many practical uses for alder leaves.

pisces

February 19 – March 20

Mutable Sign of Water ▽ Ruled by Neptune ♆

S	M	T	W	T	F	S

 Hazelwood trees surrounded the Well of Wisdom. Nine nuts fell into the well. A salmon swallowed the hazelnuts and transformed into the Salmon of Wisdom, gaining all the knowledge in the world. That is how a magical fish swam into Celtic mythology!
— Barbara Stacy

FEB. 19

WANING

Virgo

20	21	22	23	24	25	26
Sidney Poitier born, 1927	*Acquire a rose*		*Discard the unwanted*	◑		
	Libra		Scorpio		Sagittarius	

27	MARCH 1	2	3	4	5

27	28	MARCH 1	2	3	4	5
		Matronalia		*Record dreams*	●	*Visions in a pool of water*
Capricorn		Aquarius			Pisces	WAXING

6	7	8	9	10	11	12
	Love with passion	*Luther Burbank born, 1849*		*Build a friendship*		◐
Aries			Taurus		Gemini	

13	14	15	16	17	18	19
Daylight Savings Time begins @ 2am	*Use good judgement in the home*		*Rescue a cat*		Minerva's Day ⇨	Chaste Moon
	Cancer		Leo		Virgo	

20	
WANING	*Finn MacCool, apprentice to a Druid, was given the captured Salmon of Wisdom to cook. He burned his thumb and sucked the blister, transferring the wisdom. Finn MacCool became a great Irish hero, summoning powers whenever he sucked his thumb.* — Barbara Stacy

SALMON OF WISDOM

THE TRIUMPH OF ACHILLES

In the story of Patroclus
no one survives, not even Achilles
who was nearly a god.
Patroclus resembled him; they wore
the same armor.

Always in these friendships
one serves the other, one is less than the other:
the hierarchy
is always apparent, though the legends
cannot be trusted –
their source is the survivor,
the one who has been abandoned.

What were the Greek ships on fire
compared to this loss?

In his tent, Achilles
grieved with his whole being
and the gods saw
he was a man already dead, a victim
of the part that loved,
the part that was mortal.

– LOUISE GLÜCK

aries

March 20 – April 19

Cardinal Sign of Fire △ Ruled by Mars ♂

S	M	T	W	T	F	S
Mar. 20 2011 Vernal Equinox Libra	21 Bless seeds	22 Scorpio	23 Joan Crawford born, 1908	24 Travel with friends Sagittarius	25	26 ◗ Capricorn
27	28 Aquarius	29	30 Speak to the wind	31 Pisces	April 1 All Fools' Day	2 Aries
3 ● 	4 WAXING	5 Taurus	6 Prepare garden soil	7 Exercise your mind Gemini	8	9
10 Omar Sharif born, 1932 Cancer	11 ◑	12 Leo	13	14 Write a loved one Virgo	15	16 Plant seeds Libra
17 Seed Moon	18 WANING Scorpio	19				

IRON

Iron in its pure form falls from the sky as meteorites. This celestial origin resulted in its being considered a magical substance, a gift from the gods – the Egyptians credited Osiris; the Romans, Vulcan; the Teutons, Odin. Since ancient times iron has been used for protection and sometimes folk cures, a substance with healing properties used to draw out illness. Carrying some iron is believed to increase physical strength, which makes it an excellent amulet for athletes.

— ABC of Magic Charms

Alchemical symbol for iron

~ SACRED BULLS ~

WHEN ZEUS created Taurus to honor his love for Europa, the Sky Bull merged with ancient cult customs. Sacred bulls go back to a very old world, including strangely beautiful figures of these

animals on the cave walls at Lascaux. In Egypt the bull was worshipped as the spirit of Apis and sometimes Osiris. In the Sumerian *Epic of Gilgamesh*, the killing of the Bull of Heaven signaled defiance of the gods. And in Indian mythology Shiva rode Nandi the Bull, thereby sanctifying the animal.

The union of Zeus and Europa generated their own sacred bulls. Minos, their first born, became king of Crete and introduced the cult to his realm. Their early frescoes depict bull-leaping contests, essentially fertility rites, in which both men and women vault over bulls by grasping their horns. Pasiphae, the notorious wife of Minos, mated with a bull and engendered the dreaded Minotaur, a bull-headed man confined by the king to the center of a labyrinth. Each year seven young men and seven maidens were ritually sacrificed to the Minotaur until the heroic Theseus killed the creature. Today bull worship/bull sacrifice, two sides of the same coin, resonate in the arenas of Spain.

taurus
April 20 – May 19
Fixed Sign of Earth ♉ Ruled by Venus ♀

S	M	T	W	T	F	S
The Gnostic doctrine of Hermes Trismegistus, consulted by scores of medieval alchemists, was carved into what is known as the Emerald Tablet. — ABC of Magic Charms			APRIL 20 Sagittarius	21	22 Guard treasure Capricorn	23
24 Aquarius	25	26	27 Herbert Spencer born, 1820 Pisces	28 Create with color	29 Comfort a pet	30 Walpurgis Night Aries
MAY 1 Beltane	2 Honor commitments Taurus	3	4 WAXING Gemini	5	6 Support a friend	7 Plant flowers Cancer
8 White Lotus Day	9 Face your fears Leo	10	11	12 Jeddu Krishnamurti born, 1895	13 Toss three coins Libra	14
15 Scorpio	16 Vesak Day ⇨	17 Hare Moon	18 WANING Sagittarius	19 Stop bad habits	EMERALD	

Emeralds are said to protect expectant mothers and bring them safely through childbirth, strengthen memory, and help maintain chastity vows. Being attributed to Venus, the stone is a symbol of healthy romance and fulfilling love.
— ABC of Magic Charms

An emerald set en cabochon (uncut, but highly polished) was favored by European royalty during the Renaissance

The Hamsa

Healing Hand Amulet

THE SYMBOL OF THE upheld open palm has long been interpreted as healing and protective. Since ancient times pendants, murals and statues have featured the image of a helping hand. The hand held upright with the palm facing forward is a gesture that means stop. It will halt all negative influences while offering comfort. In Native American sign language, an upheld hand was an offer of peace and friendship. It suggested openness and vulnerability with no weapons in hand.

Coloring incorporated into decorative hands is part of a charm called a "hamsa." Usually bright turquoise predominates, a color especially desirable in the magical tradition of seeking divine favor. Hamsa means "five," a reference to the fingers. Hand charms are very common in the Mediterranean area. Italian, Hebrew and Arabic traditions exist involving their good powers. Sometimes the hand is considered especially sacred to Fatima, who was in early times a saint or holy maiden figure. Fatima has been called the most perfect of women. Buddha's right hand as well as the right palm of Venus appear as protective emblems to extend healing and blessings.

Jewels, designs and fabric included as part of the hand motif are thought to add to its effectiveness. The jewel, anti-evil-eye bead or other item in the center of the palm is the focal point of the hamsa. It is at the heart of the benevolent, protective energy generated by the hand.

Create your own healing hand amulet by tracing your hand on a piece of art board or cloth. Use paint, marking pens, glitter, sparkling stones, fabric, buttons or other items to create a beautiful design. Remember to include a focal point, signifying a power focus, in the center of the palm. Infused with good wishes as well as rejuvenating and protective energies, your Hamsa Hand will become a powerful amulet to display on your door, altar or other appropriate place.

– ESTHER ELAYNE

gemini

May 20 – June 20

Mutable Sign of Air △ Ruled by Mercury ☿

S	M	T	W	T	F	S
JASPER *It is believed to drive away evil spirits and not only to enhance mental functioning, but to steer the mind away from potentially harmful thought processes.* – ABC of Magic Charms					MAY 20 Capricorn	21
22 Cyril Fagan born, 1896 Aquarius	23	24 Pisces	25 Beware of enemies	26	27 Gaze into a candle flame Aries	28
29 Oak Apple Day Taurus	30	31 Partial solar eclipse ⇨	JUNE 1 Gemini	2 WAXING	3 Prepare a meal Cancer	4
5 Night of the Watchers Leo	6	7 Fashion a healing charm	8 Virgo	9 Cole Porter born, 1893	10 Libra	11 Enjoy music
12 Scorpio	13	14 Total lunar eclipse ⇨ Sagittarius	15 Dyad Moon	16 WANING Capricorn	17	18 Aquarius
19	20 Gaze at the moon	*The Egyptians associated red jasper with the blood of Isis, and in the Middle Ages it was used for medicinal purposes in cases of extensive bleeding.* – ABC of Magic Charms			*Phoenician seal cut in jasper*	

The Old Ways in Sweden

Birthing ritual in Old Sweden

THROUGHOUT SWEDEN the witch serves as custodian for ancient mystical traditions, especially those relating to the rites of passage – birth, puberty, marriage and death. A witch of Swedish descent lives in Florida and writes under the pen name Caryatid. She shares with us a birthing rite handed down through many centuries.

She tells us that once long ago, when Swedes were called Scylthings, a woman in her seventh month of pregnancy took blood from her left index finger and marked protective runes on thin strips of wood. Secretly at the full moon, she took the strips into the forest with a small cauldron, a jug of wine and one of water, salt and two pieces of linen thread, one red and one white.

After building a fire in a hollow tree and burning the wooden talismans, she carefully scooped up their ashes and mixed them with the wine. Rekindling the fire, she burned off seven-inch lengths from each strand of thread and boiled them in the cauldron of salted water. The white and red threads were hung on a limb of the tree for three days and then wrapped in clean white linen and set aside with the wine jug to await the birth.

When the child emerged and after the umbilical cord stopped throbbing, the midwife tied the linen threads a few inches apart and cut the cord between them. Outside, the wine and ashes were poured to form a circle on the ground and the baby was laid within it to absorb strength and vitality from the Earth. Incantations were addressed to the Earth Mother invoking her blessings as the child was lifted up to be acknowledged by his father. The afterbirth was buried under the same tree.

"The doctrines of Luther and the persecution of the witches of Mora in 1669 altered the rite," the witch continued. "The expectant mother in her seventh month and at the full moon burned off the lengths of red and white threads by a candle's flame and boiled them in salted water over a hearth fire. By the nineteenth century, the threads, still ritually prepared, came to be tied by the mother around the wrists of her baby – white on the left and red on the right."

A European concert pianist performing in America was recently asked why he had a red string tied around his right wrist. He answered, "My mother tied it on for good luck."

– Originally published in the 1977/1978 Witches' Almanac.

cancer
June 21 – July 21
Cardinal Sign of Water ▽ Ruled by Moon ☽

S	M	T	W	T	F	S
Moonstone is a great stone for lovers, since it is believed to arouse feelings of love. – ABC of Magic Charms	JUNE 21 Summer Solstice ☼ Pisces	22 Gather St. John's Wort	23 Aries	24 Midsummer	25 George Orwell born, 1903
26 Taurus	27 Tend the garden	28 Gemini	29	30 Partial solar eclipse ⇨ Cancer	JULY 1	2 WAXING
3 Leo	4 Carry moonstone	5 Virgo	6 Gather berries	7 Libra	8	9 Bake a pie of wishes Scorpio
10	11 Sagittarius	12	13 Set new goals Capricorn	14	15 Mead Moon	16 WANING Aquarius
17 Visit the ocean	18 Consult the tarot Pisces	19	20 Petrarch born, 1304 Aries	21		

MOONSTONE

Eastern belief holds that a living spirit actually dwells within the stone and that it is a gem of good luck. In India it is considered sacred and is never displayed for sale unless it is set upon a yellow cloth; yellow is considered an especially sacred color.

– ABC of Magic Charms

Notable Quotations

STONES

A fool can throw a stone in a pond that 100 wise men can not get out.

— *Saul Bellow*

Become dust – and they will throw thee in the air; Become stone – and they will throw thee on glass.

— *Muhammad Iqbal*

Virtue is like a rich stone, best plain set.

— *Francis Bacon*

Every block of stone has a statue inside it and it is the task of the sculptor to discover it.

— *Michelangelo*

Look at a stone cutter hammering away at his rock, perhaps a hundred times without as much as a crack showing in it. Yet at the hundred-and-first blow it will split in two, and I know it was not the last blow that did it, but all that had gone before.

— *Jacob August Riis*

The stone often recoils on the head of the thrower.

— *Elizabeth I*

Nothing is built on stone; all is built on sand, but we must build as if the sand were stone.

— *Jorge Luis Borges*

One can build from ordinary stone a humble house or the finest chateau.

— *Leon N. Cooper*

The drops of rain make a hole in the stone, not by violence, but by oft falling.

— *Lucretius*

Fling but a stone, the giant dies.

— *Matthew Green*

leo

July 22 – August 22

Fixed Sign of Fire △ Ruled by Sun ☉

LEO

S	M	T	W	T	F	S
☉ *Alchemical symbol for gold*	*Nordic myths tell of gods who kept themselves eternally young by partaking of the golden apples of Iduna, goddess of youth and spring.* – ABC of Magic Charms				JULY **22** Ancient Egyptian New Year ⇨	**23** Taurus
24	**25** Eric Hoffer born, 1902 Gemini	**26**	**27** Write a letter	**28** Cancer	**29** Listen to your dreams	**30** Leo
31 Lughnassad Eve WAXING	AUGUST **1** Lammas 🌿 Virgo	**2** Play games and feast	**3** Libra	**4** Scatter bread for the birds	**5** Scorpio	**6**
7 Sagittarius	**8** Andy Warhol born, 1931	**9** Purchase a red apple	**10** Eat a red apple Capricorn	**11**	**12** Diana's Day ⇨ Aquarius	**13** Wort Moon
14 WANING Pisces	**15**	**16**	**17** Be patient Aries	**18**	**19** Eat grapes for strength Taurus	**20**
21	**22** Gemini	GOLD *The ba is an ancient Egyptian amulet termed the "heart-soul," i.e., the soul of the physical body. It is a funereal amulet in the form of a human-headed bird made of gold and inlaid with stones.* – ABC of Magic Charms				

September

The goldenrod is yellow,
The corn is turning brown,
The trees in apple orchards
With fruit are bending down.

– HELEN HUNT JACKSON

virgo

August 23 – September 22

Mutable Sign of Earth ♍ *Ruled by Mercury* ☿

S	M	T	W	T	F	S
S A L T	(salt illustration)	Aug. 23	24 Jorge Luis Borges born, 1899 Cancer	25 Buy salt for use in magic	26 Leo	27 Harvest corn
28 ● Virgo	29 WAXING	30 Libra	31 Sing!	Sept. 1 Ganesh Festival Scorpio	2	3 Be aware of ghosts
4 ◐ Sagittarius	5 Challenge stale concepts	6 Capricorn	7	8 Aquarius	9 Avoid a conflict	10
11 Pisces	12 Barley Moon	13 WANING Aries	14 Use caution when travelling	15	16 Honor tradition Taurus	17
18 Gemini	19 Keep your own opinions	20 ◑	21 Leonard Cohen born, 1934 Cancer	22 Remember old friends		

Since ancient times spilling salt requires throwing a pinch over your shoulder to ward off any hovering demons. Buddhist tradition calls for the same observance to ward off bad spirits before entering a house observing a funeral. Sumo wrestlers throw a handful of salt into the ring before they enter, again to ward off unwelcome invisible visitors. In 1933 the previous Dalai Lama was entombed sitting up to his neck in salt. Still today salt may be used as a purifying sacrament, and a gift of salt portends good luck.

– ABC of Magic Charms

TAROT'S LOVERS

THE LOVERS.

Rider-Waite-Smith deck

THE LOVERS represents the sixth card of the Major Arcana, its symbols suggesting the biblical Genesis. Two nude figures, unveiled as for all verity, bring to mind Adam and Eve as they first encounter themselves in the Earthly Garden. Their harmonious aspects suggest youth, virginity and innocence – love uncontaminated by lust. Behind the male is the Tree of Life, bearing twelve fruits; behind the female, the Knowledge of Good and Evil tree holding a twining serpent. The Sun shines at high noon, consciousness at its fullest. A looming angel with flaming hair and wings, arms extended, pours down influences.

The Lovers represent the impulse that drives us out of the Garden toward adulthood, prompting the querent to examine relationships and choices. The card may indicate a decision about an existing love, a new temptation or potential partnership. A bachelor's lifestyle may have to be sacrificed for a settled relationship or vice versa, and one partner may be chosen and another turned down. Choices must be attended by the utmost seriousness.

libra
September 23 – October 22
Cardinal Sign of Air ♎ Ruled by Venus ♀

LIBRA

S	M	T	W	T	F	S
Jade is highly revered by the Chinese and is used in several talismans of good luck. – ABC of Magic Charms			SHOU – *Chinese sign of longevity*		Sept. **23** Autumnal Equinox Leo	**24**
25 Virgo	**26** *Make a wish for love*	**27** Libra	**28** WAXING	**29** *J.B. Rhine born, 1895* Scorpio	**30**	Oct. **1** *Learn a new dance* Sagittarius
2	**3** Capricorn	**4** *Seek a pet's affection*	**5** Aquarius	**6**	**7** *Write poetry*	**8** Pisces
9	**10** *Perform fire gazing* Aries	**11** Blood Moon	**12** WANING	**13** Taurus	**14** *Dine with a lover*	**15** *Virgil born, 70 BCE* Gemini
16	**17**	**18** *Avoid shadows* Cancer	**19**	**20** *Cast a spell* Leo	**21**	**22** *Gather oak leaves* Virgo

JADE

Jade takes its name from the Spanish piedra de ijada, *which means "stone of the flank." In addition, one variety of jade is called nephrite, from the Greek* nephros, *meaning kidney. So not surprisingly, jade is believed to cure ailments of the groin and kidneys.*

– ABC of Magic Charms

YEAR OF THE METAL RABBIT
February 3, 2011 to January 22, 2012

THROUGHOUT the Orient, the gentle Rabbit or Hare is a welcome message bearer. This year promises a comparatively peaceful cycle following the feisty Tiger. Creative urges, logical problem solving, a kindly demeanor, and clear-cut goals make life more comfortable. Sensible and suave, the congenial Metal Rabbit's expectation to acquire the best of everything is often fulfilled. Rabbit's legendary flexibility is in evidence. There is a tendency to play both sides against the middle successfully and still remain on cordial terms with all involved.

The Oriental astrology cycle follows a pattern of twelve years. Five elements: fire, water, wood, metal, and earth are incorporated in a sixty-year pattern. Then the element–animal pairs repeat. Chinese New Year begins at the second New Moon following the winter solstice, in late January to mid-February. It almost always coincides with the New Moon in Aquarius in the familiar Western zodiac. Legend teaches that Rabbit was the fourth animal rewarded with its own year for answering an invitation to a party hosted by the Buddha.

Those born during a Rabbit year are gifted with longevity, as well as a refined and virtuous nature. The well-mannered, unassuming and scholarly Rabbit is a much sought-after partner in both marriage and business relationships. Respected for artistic ability and sensitivity, Rabbit practices discretion in all things.

Those born during a Rabbit year, as listed below, can anticipate a new cycle of growth. Jump out of the burrow and explore the great possibilities that are about to present themselves.

Chinese Chance! Chinese New Year begins with the second New Moon after the winter solstice. It occurs in late January to mid-February, not on January 1. For January and February births, check to make certain which animal sign corresponds. It might be the one for the previous year for those births taking place before Chinese New Year.

1915, 1927, 1939, 1951, 1963, 1975, 1987, 1999, 2011

Illustration by Ogmios MacMerlin

scorpio

October 23 – November 21

Fixed Sign of Water ▽ Ruled by Pluto ♀

ʃCORPIVʃ

S	M	T	W	T	F	S
Oct. 23	24 *Beware of insect bites* Libra	25 *Johann Strauss born, 1825*	26 ● Scorpio	27 WAXING	28 *Judge no one* Sagittarius	29
30 *Light a white candle* Capricorn	31 *Samhain Eve*	Nov. 1 Hallowmas	2 ◑ Aquarius	3	4 *Ancestors speak to descendants* Pisces	5 *View old photographs*
6 *Daylight Savings Time ends @ 2am*	7 Aries	8	9 *Visit a cemetery* Taurus	10 ◯ Snow Moon	11 WANING	12 Gemini
13	14 *Jawaharlel Nehru born, 1889* Cancer	15 *Bake a pie*	16 *Hecate Night* Leo	17 *Earn respect*	18 ◐	19 Virgo
20	21 *Taste a chocolate* Libra					

BLOODSTONE

In an Egyptian document that dates to the 3rd century CE, bloodstone receives the following praise for its amuletic properties: "The world has no greater thing; if any one have this with him he will be given whatever he asks for; it also assuages the wrath of kings and despots, and whatever the wearer says will be believed. Whoever bears this stone, which is a gem, and pronounces the name engraved upon it, will find all doors open, while bonds and stone walls will be rent asunder."

– ABC of Magic Charms

A medieval jeweler suggests using bloodstone to prevent nosebleed

Uzume

Goddess of holy hilarity

HERE we have the bawdiest divinity in the international pantheon. Uzume is a Shinto goddess dedicated to joy, ribald jokes, raucous laughter and licentious dancing. Such disorderly conduct turns up to good purpose in ancient Japanese stories. Her central myth tells us how Uzume's shocking, shocking, behavior restored sunlight to a dark world.

The sun goddess Amaterasu, the Great Woman Who Possesses Noon, had a depraved brother justly known as the Outrageous Male. Susanowo was jealous of his sister's glory. He broke into the Weaving Hall of Heaven, over which Amaterasu presided, shouting, smashing and desecrating with filth the sacred silk looms. The weaving priestesses fled screaming.

Undone by uproar, the sun goddess retreated to the Sky-Rock-Cave and sealed the door with a boulder. Quiet, solitude. Solace. But darkness and infertility befell the world. Eight hundred deities gathered at the cave to deal with the calamity. They tried to lure her out with glittering presents, which they hung on a sacred sakaki tree to no avail.

Uzume stepped up in classic mind-if-I-try mode. She rolled up her sleeves, attached bells to ankles and wrists, and climbed atop a tub. The odd goddess, whose name means "Whirler," began dancing drum rhythms, singing, and shouting ribald jokes. The story comes down to us from a seventh-century chronicle which unfortunately neglected to note the jokes. The excited deities joined the commotion, shouting with laughter.

Suddenly Uzume bared her breasts, and before the gods and goddesses recovered from that maneuver, the Whirler threw her kimono up over her waist. The gesture was so in the spirit of over-the-top jest that the laughter increased to screaming hilarity. Amaterasu became curious about the commotion. She decided to peek out the door, but one god had replaced the boulder with a bronze mirror. Amaterasu's reflected light was so dazzling that she could see nothing. She stepped outside and the gods quickly sealed the cave. Once again light and warmth blessed our planet.

sagittarius

November 22 – December 20

Mutable Sign of Fire △ Ruled by Jupiter ♃

S	M	T	W	T	F	S
Sumerian kings and queens fashioned cylinder seals from lapis; the Egyptians carved scarabs. – ABC of Magic Charms		Nov. 22	23 *Deep thoughts* Scorpio	24 Partial solar eclipse ⇨	25 ● Sagittarius	26 WAXING
27 *Hold a sacred object* Capricorn	28	29 *Amos B. Alcott born, 1799* Aquarius	30 *Reread an old book*	Dec. 1 Pisces	2 ◐	3 *Clean house*
4 Aries	5	6 *Dave Brubeck born, 1920* Taurus	7 *Whisper desires into a shell*	8 *Watch your temper*	9 *Total lunar eclipse ⇨* Gemini	10 Oak Moon
11 WANING Cancer	12 *Contact spirits*	13	14 Leo	15 *Enchant a broom*	16 *Fairy Queen Eve* Virgo	17 ◑ Saturnalia
18 *Take time with familiars* Libra	19	20 Scorpio				

Lapis Lazuli

...a gold-flecked blue stone so beautiful that it is believed gods actually rejoice in inhabiting it and bestowing potent magical powers upon its wearer. The Chinese carve a traditional design of pomegranate and a bat on the blue stone to assure its wearer of a long, full, and successful life. Japanese of the Shinto faith choose lapis lazuli as the gem upon which to engrave the crane symbol called tsuru, for good luck.

– ABC of Magic Charms

TSURU – Japanese crane of good luck

New Year's Traditions

Sweet grape, sweet month;
sour grape, sour month

AT THE stroke of midnight in Italy, Portugal, Spain and countries to which their people have emigrated, a curious custom is observed. As the witching hour approaches, everyone eats twelve grapes, one for each month of the year. In Peru, celebrants eat a thirteenth grape for luck.

Some people make a wish on each grape, some speak the name of the month aloud. Some even note the taste of the grape corresponding to each month – sweet grape, sweet month; sour grape, sour month. Others try to eat each grape before the next bell peals, washing the last one down with champagne.

Why grapes? In 1909 a grape surplus arose in the Alicante region of Spain. Merchants needed to sell a surplus of grapes and apparently invented the custom, which continues. Despite the mercenary origins of the tradition, it's an appropriate one. At the New Year, rituals are observed to secure luck and prosperity in the coming year. Grapes, round to oblong, look like miniature eggs – and eggs serve as an ancient symbol of fertility. Down the centuries, a fertile, multiplying flock of hens was prosperity.

Whether the grape growers of the early twentieth century knew it or not, they had started a magically sound tradition. Even raisins, the dried form of grapes, represent a full harvest. One family group in Portugal substitutes raisins for grapes.

Lentils are another common food eaten for prosperity in the new year. They are thought to resemble coins in both their shape and their occasional yellow color. In parts of Italy and in Italian-American enclaves, the lentil custom is still observed in delicious form – cooked into a rich stew with sausages. In Brazil, lentils turn up as soup or over rice.

Other food customs abound according to ethnic beliefs. On New Year's Eve, one family tradition is to serve beef and pork, but not poultry or fish. Tradition says that the hooves of pigs and cows point forward, but chickens scratch backward and fish can swim backward, making them unfit symbols for moving ahead in the new year.

Even the store-bought snacks and finger foods served at New Year's parties have their purpose. One tradition holds that whatever you are doing at the start of the New Year portends the whole year, and what could be better than being surrounded by bounty, sharing, and friendship?

– MORVEN WESTFIELD

capricorn
December 21 – January 19
Cardinal Sign of Earth ▽ Ruled by Saturn ♄

S	M	T	W	T	F	S
leað *Lead and the color black were representative of Saturn's supposed dark and malefic qualities...* – ABC of Magic Charms			Dec. **21** Winter Solstice ❄	**22** Sagittarius	**23** *Store mistletoe*	**24** ● Capricorn
25 WAXING	**26**	**27** *Keep warm* Aquarius	**28**	**29** *Pablo Casals born, 1876* Pisces	**30** *Carry a mirror – avoid a curse*	**31** Aries
Jan. **1** ◑ 2012	**2** *State year's goals*	**3** *Cicero born, 106 BCE* Taurus	**4**	**5** *Be patient* Gemini	**6**	**7**
8 Feast of Janus ⇨ Cancer	**9** (Wolf Moon)	**10** WANING Leo	**11**	**12** Virgo	**13** *Celebrate*	**14** Libra
15	**16** ◐ Scorpio	**17** *Wear red for power*	**18** Sagittarius	**19**		

4	9	2
3	5	7
8	1	6

♄ *Alchemical symbol for lead*

The Magic Square of Saturn – nine figures adding up vertically, horizontally, and diagonally to total fifteen – was engraved on a sheet of lead and carried as an amulet. Today lead is often employed as a protective token and used to guard valuables.

– ABC of Magic Charms

Urania, 1502. *Urania, the muse of astronomy, holding an armillary sphere with zodiac.*

The Universe is full of magical things,
patiently waiting for our wits to grow sharper.

– EDEN PHILPOTTS

aquarius

January 20 – February 18

Fixed Sign of Air △ Ruled by Uranus ♅

S	M	T	W	T	F	S
SODALITE *This most beautiful stone will fluoresce under ultraviolet light. Darkness will also restore its brilliance, also accelerated by ultraviolet light.* – ABC of Magic Charms					Jan. 20	21 *Look toward the future* Capricorn
22	23 **Year of the Dragon** Aquarius	24 WAXING	25 *Undines are angered* Pisces	26 *Eartha Kitt born, 1928*	27	28 Aries
29	30 🌓	31 *Step on a silver coin* Taurus	Feb. 1 *Oimelc Eve*	2 Candlemas Gemini	3 *Contemplate*	4 Cancer
5 *Melt snow in your hands*	6 Leo	7 *Storm Moon*	8 WANING Virgo	9 *Drink water by moonlight*	10	11 *Virginia E. Johnson born, 1925* Libra
12	13 *Make runes* Scorpio	14 🌗	15 Lupercalia Sagittarius	16	17 *Have a party* Capricorn	18

Sodalite inspires thoughts as deep as its color and encourages understanding through higher thinking. The stone is excellent for the seeker of wisdom, calming its wearer and promoting deep meditation leading to a balance of thought and spirit.

– ABC of Magic Charms

KITCHEN MAGIC

How Sweet It Is!

EVERYONE SEEMS TO love sweet potato pie, with its moist-fleshed, gently spicy flavor, appealing aroma and cheerful color. Throughout the South, such a delicious pie is part of every cook's repertory, sometimes as side dish, sometimes as dessert – the ingredients are similar. For the rest of the country, too often we remember sweet potatoes and their versatility during the winter holidays. But sweet potatoes and yams, their bright orange version, are available in most markets year-long.

Sweet potatoes are native to Central America, one of the most ancient foods known to man. Relics ten thousand years old have been found in Peruvian caves. Columbus brought them back to Europe and today few parts of the world are strangers to the sweet natures of these root veggies.

Once you have sweet potatoes at home, refrain from refrigerator storage. Remove from the bag and arrange them loosely in a dark cool place, ideally a cupboard away from the stove, where they should keep fresh for up to ten days. Once cooked, sweet potato leftovers may be refrigerated, although in the case of sweet potato pie remains are seldom a problem.

Sweet Potato Pie

2 medium (about 1 1/2 pounds) sweet
   potatoes, washed and unpeeled
4 tablespoons melted butter
1/2 cup each brown sugar and
   white sugar
1/3 cup honey
2 eggs, well beaten
1/2 teaspoon each ground ginger
   and cloves
1/4 teaspoon nutmeg
1 cup evaporated milk or half-and-half
1 cup pecans (optional)
1 9-inch unbaked pie shell

Cover the potatoes in a pan with water, bring to a boil and reduce heat to medium. Cook for about 45 minutes or until potatoes are soft. Drain, cool and peel. Mash the potatoes well with the butter, sugars and honey. Add the eggs and spices, blending well. Stir in half-and-half or milk and blend well. Pour the mixture into the crust and sprinkle the top with the pecans, if desired (some may sink, that is okay). Bake for 10 minutes at 400°, reduce heat to 350° and bake for 30 minutes, or until the center is firm and a small knife inserted in the center comes out clean. Cool on a rack until just warm. If desired for dessert pie, serve with a scoop of vanilla ice cream or whipped cream.

pisces

February 19 – March 20

Mutable Sign of Water ▽ *Ruled by Neptune* ♆

S	M	T	W	T	F	S
Feb. 19 Aquarius	20 Turn a curse	21 ●	22 WAXING Pisces	23	24 Recite a rhyme Aries	25 Meher Baba born, 1894
26	27 Taurus	28 Leap Year Day ⇨	29 ◑ Gemini	March 1 Matronalia	2 Hold a love's hand Cancer	3 Mix sea, rain and river waters
4	5 Leo	6 Michelangelo born, 1475	7 Spot a rabbit for good luck Virgo	8 Chaste Moon	9 WANING Libra	10
11 Daylight Savings Time begins @ 2am Scorpio	12	13 Stay clear of fires Sagittarius	14 ◑	15 Capricorn	16 Climb a hill	17 Aquarius
18 Read poetry	19 Minerva's Day Pisces	20				

AMETHYST

It was the jewel to the late 10th century worn by the High Priest during the initiation rites into the Eleusinian Mysteries in order that he might not become "confused, distracted or overwhelmed by the intense fascination of external phenomena." The secrets of Eleusis were never revealed, and eventually Dionysos, the god of wine, was worshipped there.

– ABC of Magic Charms

The Lorscher Ring, a dark purple amethyst set in gold is a treasured German antiquity dated to the late 10th century

The Three Kings

A Cosmic Trio of Fixed Stars

Alnitak (24 Gemini 01), Alnilam (22 Gemini 04), Mintaka (22 Gemini 24)

FOR thousands of years distinctive earthly landscape features have been linked with messages hinted at by fixed-star patterns in the heavens. Both naturally occurring and manmade structures mirror the cosmic messages spelled out in the distant twinkling canopy of stars which oversees life on Earth. The Great Pyramids of Giza in Egypt (built almost five thousand years ago by the Pharaoh-Kings); Bird Mound at Poverty Point, Louisiana; Ohio's Serpent Mound; Machu Picchu in Peru and the ancient observatory at Chichen Itza in Mexico's Yucatan Peninsula are just a few examples.

Intriguing places also exist which might be either naturally occurring or manmade. Encoded within mountains, stones, canyons and lakes all around the world are more patterns accurately reflecting stars and constellations. Among these a grouping of three rocks off the coast of Scotland, in the Firth of Forth, is especially captivating. The rocks might be manmade or naturally occurring volcanic structures. Named Lamb, Craigleith and Fidra, the Islands, like the three Great Pyramids of Giza, precisely trace the exact meandering line of the stars known as the Three Kings in the constellation Orion. Not only the pyramids, but the Three Kings of Celtic myth, including Arthur, Robert the Bruce and various ancient Irish Kings, are honored in the legends linked to these three sacred stones.

Ley lines connecting the Islands to Tara, Bannockburn, Stonehenge, Rosslyn Chapel and Glastonbury suggest a complex relationship to ancient prophecies revealed by the stars. Lamb Island has a reference to the term Lamb of God, showing an affinity with Jesus. A fifteenth-century manuscript, the

"Scotichronichon," by an Abbot of Inchcolm, states that the rocks where Noah's Ark came to rest may be here. The true location of the Isle of Avalon, where Arthur was laid to rest, is often linked to these three sacred islands by other scholars. Prince Gaytheolos and Princess Scota, ancient founders of Scotland, first found refuge here too, according to some beliefs.

The Three Kings are a twinkling stellar brotherhood. They are named Alnitak (24 Gemini 01), Alnilam (22 Gemini 04) and Mintaka (22 Gemini 24). Alnitak, the most eastern, is white and violet, with a nature of Mercury. Alnilam, in the center, is white with a fortunate nature expressing Jupiter and Saturn. Mintaka, on the western edge, is variable, pale violet and also expresses a fortunate Mercurial/Jovian nature. The stars' Arabic names are variations on translations of words for "girdle" or "belt." Together the three stars form the distinctive belt worn by Orion, the giant heavenly hunter. Orion was once thought to have been created from an ox hide by three gods, Mercury, Neptune and Jupiter, as a hospitality gift for Hyreus following a memorable evening of entertainment.

The Three Kings stars create a stunning picture in the night sky. Usually their interpretation by astrologers has been masculine. In Australia they were viewed as three handsome men dancing to celestial music played by the Pleiades sisters, a grouping of stars in nearby Taurus. In Greenland they became three seal hunters, in Germany three harvesters. In China they were seen as part of a weighing beam, while in Southern Europe they became the three staffs of Jacob, Peter and Mary. Further north the trio is linked to the Magi, or the Three Wise Men. The line they make has been called at various times a girdle of pearls, golden grains, nuts or spangles. In medieval astrology a devotion to hunting is seen in Orion and his trio of stars. Alfred Lord Tennyson honored them with these famous lines:

> *These three stars of the*
> *airy giant's zone*
>
> *That glitter burnished*
> *by the frosty dark.*

> – DIKKI-JO MULLEN

The Three Kings
in individual horoscopes

ALL THOSE born from June 10-19 of any year have the Three Kings in conjunction with the natal Sun. A cautious and discreet nature, public honors, preferment and gain, and changeability are the traits they offer.

Check for other planets from 19 to 27 degrees of Gemini in individual horoscopes. According to the planet involved, the Three Kings will be influential in a positive way.

Keynotes for The Three Kings
in conjunction with the current 2011-2012 transits:

With the South Node from May – August 2011: Studious influences, interesting publications and lawsuits can come to the forefront. Showdowns between adversaries are more blatant.

With Mars – The last half of July, 2011: Energy levels will be higher; conversations become lively debates. This is a wonderful time for brainstorming.

With the Lunar Eclipse (at the Full Moon) of December 10, 2011: Business trends will be important indicators of the future. Public figures experience changes in status. Education is accented.

(An orb of about three degrees is used in noting the influence of fixed stars. They are traditionally considered only influential when in the conjunction aspect to a planet or luminary.)

– DIKKI JO MULLEN

Window on the Weather

PLANETARY ALIGNMENT determines the center of gravity in our solar system, a key factor in determining the amount of energy radiated by the sun and which regulates the temperature of Earth to a surprising degree. The current configuration has reduced the amount of sunspots to near record minimum and is responsible for much of the severe cold recorded in recent years in Europe and South America. This development has also caused Earth's magnetic field to become thin. Moreover, the stratosphere near the North Pole is warming: this pattern can bring cold to the Northeast United States during the summer. In this instance, it is best understood that past is prologue. Similar patterns through the centuries have lead on occasions to mini ice ages. It behooves us to expect the unexpected.

– Tom C. Lang

SPRING

MARCH 2011. March brings energy to the atmosphere, with some of nature's greatest storms occurring during this month. While the average daily temperature rises at the greatest rate nationwide, the potential for copious snowfall remains high, especially throughout interior New England, the Northern Plains, and western mountains. With heavy snowfalls in the Sierra Nevada, water supply in the West should remain ample. Dry conditions are anticipated in the Southeast increasing threat of fires in Florida where unseasonably warm weather is also expected. Tornado season arrives in the Mississippi Valley with an outbreak of potentially severe weather from Oklahoma to Alabama. Spring tornadoes often strike at night and a weather radio is a fine investment in these areas.

APRIL 2011. A dry spring is anticipated in the East with cooler than average temperatures in New England. Occasionally, temperatures rise briefly to summer levels before again turning colder. Sunshine remains abundant farther south, including Florida. Farther west, cold weather is slow to retreat from Chicago to the Northern Plains. Tornadoes are more numerous but isolated in scope. Late season snowfall is heavy in the Northern Rockies. West Coast rain and wind sweeps the California coastline, also drenching Portland and Seattle whereas Texas and the Gulf Coast states are quite dry.

MAY 2011. Annually, the greatest number of tornadoes occur in May and are primarily focused in Oklahoma and Texas. In fact, Oklahoma City is the metropolitan location most frequently struck by these powerful storms. Tornadoes most often occur between approximately 3pm to 8pm, although, theoretically, they may occur any time. Though less common elsewhere, twisters have been recorded in every state. Smaller "Tornado Alleys" also exist in central New England, California's central valleys, central Colorado, and the Ohio Valley. Tornado frequency should be somewhat more widespread this month.

SUMMER

JUNE 2011. Hot, dry weather blankets the East with only New England experiencing cooler than average temperatures. Conditions there are dry with only occasional thunderstorms experienced from Michigan to the Northeast. Temperatures commonly reach the 90s in the Southeast and mid-Atlantic. Meanwhile, the West remains cold with sparse rainfall limited to the mountains. Arkansas, Texas, and Oklahoma may expect severe thunderstorms while several outbreaks of tornadoes may sweep the Dakotas and Minnesota. High country camping in the West is limited as the snowpack is slow to melt.

JULY 2011. The warmest time of the year in the Northern Hemisphere occurs about a month following the Summer Solstice, usually in late July, and relates to Earth's continued absorption of solar warmth into August. Weather systems move slowly, resulting in longer lasting late day thunderstorms throughout the East and mountainous West. Sea breezes become feeble along the ocean edge. Temperatures of land and sea are similar. Thunderstorms are a daily event on the west coast of Florida as well as near Orlando. Isolated tornadoes are confined to the northern border of the United States.

AUGUST 2011. Hot weather becomes less oppressive, as the sun's rays become less direct. Still, even on hazy days, sunburn remains a risk and appropriate sunscreen protection guidelines should be followed. The tropical Atlantic stirs to life with the season's first hurricane activity. The most vulnerable areas for such a storm are the Gulf Coast and Southeast United States. Daily showers fall along the Western Continental Divide. New England is cooler than average as are the Northern Rockies, while the southern Plains swelter in excessive heat.

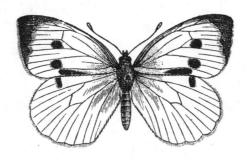

AUTUMN

SEPTEMBER 2011. September represents the peak of tropical storm season: anticipate approximately six hurricanes and two major storms with perhaps one that makes landfall. Most perilous are "Cape Verde" hurricanes, which form near those islands near the coast of Africa and which may gather energy and generate powerful winds for over a week while crossing the Atlantic basin. Conditions for such storms ease by the 20th. Otherwise, September is a relatively dry month nationwide with little or no rain at lower elevations. In the East, the approach of chilly autumn temperatures quickens by the 30th as several cold fronts pass.

OCTOBER 2011. Fall colors advance from north to south, beginning around the 7th with the maple trees of northern New England and reaching the southern Appalachians by the 25th. First frost is felt in the Northern Rockies and Minnesota by the 20th, as polar air moves south. Generally dry conditions are expected in the East, whereas rainfall is abundant in the Mississippi Valley. The Southeast remains hotter than average and late season hurricanes may threaten south Florida. The Cascade Mountains in the Pacific Northwest experience a dusting of snow.

NOVEMBER 2011. Western New York may experience a minor dusting of snow. Crisp temperatures are also felt in New England and points south along the Eastern Seaboard. The first Pacific storms arrive in the Northwest with several days of wind-driven rain from Seattle to San Francisco. Conditions warn of high fire danger in southern California with the appearance of the Santa Ana winds. Florida turns cooler; the result of a welcome passing cold front that yields rain showers and eases potential fire danger. The Great Plains and Ohio valley are cool and dry.

WINTER

DECEMBER 2011. Arctic cold returns to New England, with snowfall along the Mid-Atlantic. By the 15th, a light snow cover likely extends from Central New England, west through the Great Lakes where heavier snowfalls occur. The Tennessee Valley experiences frost. Snowfall is heavy near Denver, promising a fine skiing season. El Niño having waned, the Sierra Nevada experiences below average snowfall and the Pacific Coast enjoys beautiful weather. Florida also enjoys exceptional weather, with little evidence of severe weather and the termination of hurricane season.

JANUARY 2012. While the southeast United States remains relatively mild, the Northeast, Great Lakes states, and mountainous west is colder than average. A series of disturbances bring moderate snowfalls to southern New England and the Ohio Valley. Lake-effect snow is heavy this year near Buffalo and Syracuse, New York.

Chicago and Minneapolis experience temperatures that remain below zero for several days. In the West, seasonably cold air settles along the coast with San Francisco enjoying sunshine and temperatures in the 50s. Snowfall increases in the Sierra Nevada. Nationwide the coldest week of the year occurs by the 25th, though freezing temperatures are not especially likely in Florida. Snowfall is also above normal in the lower Ohio Valley.

FEBRUARY 2012. February snowfall is heavy in the Northeast and Eastern Great Lakes, reversing a trend in recent years. Boston and New York may be especially hard hit and high storm winds may also cause some localized coastal damage. Temperatures are close to average nationally with the exceptions of Southern California and Florida which are somewhat warmer than usual. Both these areas are also particularly dry. Rain showers keep the Pacific Northwest green and snowfall is heavy from the Cascades to the northern Sierra Nevada. Lengthening days aid snow removal. Atlanta may be visited by a modest snow event. Thunderstorm activity is confined to the Gulf Coast.

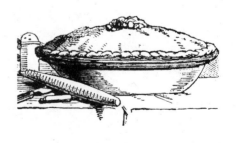

Orisha Oko

Divinity of the earth's fruits

THE YORUBA of Southwestern Nigeria have long honored the earth as not only the source of their very being but also the space upon which they set the altars to their deities, the Orisha. Out of the earth mankind was born and into the earth many of the Orisha were absorbed. It is no wonder that chief among their deities is the divinity of farming and their staple food, Orisha Oko. It is he who the honors of the first of the harvest are given and it is to him that many look to for not only fertility of the land but also fertility of the body.

The great yam festival

Iyan, pounded yams, is the staple starch without which a meal would not be complete. Not only is this a staple of mankind, it is also a primary offering to the Orisha. To Orisha Oko falls the most important of festivals – the harvest festival that marks the beginning of the year. As the rainy season comes and the year draws to a close, the priests of Oko begin to prepare for the festival, his grand festival.

The first preparations of the festival begin with the disposing of the yams that are still in storage. A new year can not be marked with the old, but only the new. The priests will supervise the disposition of the old yams so that the new harvest will not bear the bitterness of old yams. With the old gone and homes cleaned of all old harvested foods, the priest will set about supervising the harvest of the new yams. This is the most sacred of tasks. Many offerings of kola nuts and fresh water will be made to Orisha Oko, thanking him for bringing fertility to land and to families over the past year, as well as prayers for the year to come.

A procession of priests will go to the field to make the first of the harvest. It is there in the fields that the priests will split one of the newly harvested yams into four pieces. They will throw these onto the ground and read the light and dark to ascertain whether Orisha Oko is pleased with the offerings and prayers made and whether the coming year will bring many children and further good harvests.

Before the festivities of dancing and feasting begin the priests will make their final act by bringing the first of the yams to be offered Orisha Oko in his shrine and to the ancestors. Among the principal attendees at the shrine will be the regional king or the eldest man in the community. And it is to them that the first yams are offered for eating after Oko has been properly propitiated. It is through their intercession that the other divinities and ancestors partake of the feast.

Earth fertility, body fertility

In Yorubaland Orisha Oko's shrine is dominated by his staff. It is divided into three sections for his various roles in the divine scheme. The bottom third is shaped like a blade and is reminiscent of his role as the tiller of land. The middle third of the staff is made of wood, reminding us that foods to eat can not only be found on the tilled land but can also be harvested from the forest that surround the farms. The top third of the staff is shaped like a stylized penis and connects him with not only fertility of the land but the fertility of the body.

Orisha Oko's connection with the dual fertility of body and land is explicitly expressed in his name. The name Oko has many meanings. Oko can mean husband and in the strongly male-dominated society of the Yorubas, it is the husband that brings fertility to his wife. Oko can also mean farm, and given his association with the farm this is not surprising. Lastly Oko can also mean penis. In fact, one of his many praise names is *Eni-duru* which translates as "erect person," immediately reminding again that he is associated with the erect penis and fertility.

In Cuba and the Caribbean, the Diaspora's Orisha Oko shrine points more literally to the farming and fertility. His shrine is dominated by a statue of two oxen pulling a plow with a farmer behind them. The shrine is also occupied by two coconuts that have been painted red and white. These point to fertility experienced in the Caribbean through the fecundity of the coconut palm. They are also reminiscent of testicles, reminding us that in many stories about him, his scrotum is said to drag on the floor.

Orisha Oko is associated with all forms of farming. This even extends to his special messengers, bees and his other sacred food. Like humans they cultivate, creating honey through their careful selection from plants.

Orisha Oko and the birds

Orisha Oko has many stories associated with him. A story which is a favorite among the folk Irawo, the land of his birth and where he is heavily worshipped, is related here:

Orisa Oko was a farmer from Irawo who was known to his town people as a man learned in medicines, leaves and herbs.

One year, there appeared three large blackbirds that landed on the field in Irawo that wreaked havoc and ate all 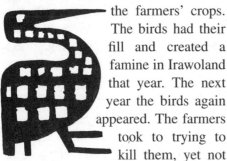 the farmers' crops. The birds had their fill and created a famine in Irawoland that year. The next year the birds again appeared. The farmers took to trying to kill them, yet not a single arrow would pierce their body or bring harm to them. The town people, knowing that Orisha Oko was wise in many ways, decided to ask to use his medicine to help bring the end to the birds.

Orisha Oko prepared a powerful medicine that was able to drive the birds away. With the departure of the birds, the crops were again able to grow and that year there was realized the biggest harvest. The town people were immensely happy and grateful to Orisha Oko, so much so that they made him their king.

As time went by, the town people began to realize a fear of their new king. They believed that if his medicine could rid them of the birds, perhaps he could use his medicine against any whom he did not like. They grew more and more fearful and eventually were suspicious of him. And although they prospered and he gave them no cause for complaint, their fear grew so much that one day they rose up in revolt and drove him out of the town.

The following year, however, at harvest time, the birds returned again bringing with them famine, causing the crops to fail. It was then that the people realized their mistake and went off to find Orisha Oko. They found him in short order in the forest and begged him to return once more to help them by ridding them of the birds. All the town people told him that they would again like him to be their king and promised to never again rise up against him. But this time Orisha Oko could not be swayed. He said he could not rule a people who would harbor ill thoughts and distrust. But he did take pity on them, saying, "I will leave you forever, but I shall leave my sword behind. Any time you are in real danger, you may thrust the sword into the ground, and I will come and protect the crops. But do not use it lightly or in vain."

Once he finished his instructions, Orisha Oko disappeared into the ground. His sword, however, is still found stuck in the ground in his shrine where he disappeared.

In Orisha Oko we find the father of agriculture, who provides us with sustenance through our life. And at the end of life, we provide sustenance to him by giving our body back to the earth.

– Ifadoyin Sangomuyiwa
Nigerian Priest to Sango and Babalawo, Father of Secrets

Ifadoyin lives in New Jersey, where he also maintains a spiritual house. He can be contacted directly, through his website www.irunmole.org.

Circe's Torment

I regret bitterly
The years of loving you in both
Your presence and absence, regret
The law, my vocation
That forbid me to keep you, the sea
A sheet of glass, the sun-bleached
Beauty of the Greek ships: how
Could I have power if
I had no wish
To transform you: as
You loved my body,
As you found there
Passion we held above
All other gifts, in that single moment
Over honor and hope, over
Loyalty, in the name of that bond
I refuse you
Such feeling for your wife
As will let you
Rest with her, I refuse you
Sleep again
If I cannot have you.

– LOUISE GLÜCK

69

Gravestone Rubbings

Funerary treasures

THESE DAYS we take little time at cemeteries for funerals and Memorial Day obligations, like visits to unpleasant relatives. But attitudes can change. In the nineteenth century cemeteries were designed like parks, their landscapes destinations for family picnics or nightly walks. In the 1970's the popularity of genealogy sparked an appreciation of funerary folk art and created a newfound respect for the culture, art and history offered by gravestones.

Since then, tombstone images have spread beyond the graveyard and toured the country through collections of rubbings and plaster casts. Such re-creations have become recognized as fascinating art forms. Gravestone designs are silkscreened on shirts, published in books, shown in museums and mounted on the walls of homes, many in places of honor reserved for relatives and ancestors.

Rubbings inspire both positive and negative responses. Some states have banned this process because of permanent damage to tombstones, while other places welcome the technique to preserve life-sized replicas.

It is clear that the process requires the right tools and a healthy dose of respect.

The simplest and safest way to make a rubbing is the same method we learned as children. By putting a leaf or penny under paper, we ran the sides of a crayon back and forth to create a relief of the object underneath.

No attempts should ever be made to make rubbings of flaking, crumbling or lichen-covered stones that might sustain further damage. The best method to preserve the design in this situation is to take a photograph. Cameras often capture images that can't be distinguished at a location. Sometime detail can be brought out further in sandstone or granite by wetting it.

Gravestone rubbing is not quick and free of effort, but care will pay off. Carvings that are well defined but not deeply cut make the best candidates for rubbing. You can further ensure your success by preparing a kit to take along:

→ small notebook, pen and paper clips
→ camera
→ soft-bristle fingernail brush
→ soft toothbrush
→ popsicle stick
→ spray bottle of water
→ absorbent cloth
→ scissors
→ masking tape
→ charcoal, blackboard chalk, rubbing wax or black lumber-yard crayon (used to temporarily mark lumber)
→ thin, tough, wide paper or heavy, nonfusible interface cloth
→ trash bag
→ snack or lunch, including water
→ container for carrying supplies
→ construction tool apron (optional)

Before beginning, record details about your stone's location, inscription and design. Brush away debris with soft nylon brushes. Use a popsicle stick to clean out its engravings. Anything still attached can then be sprayed with water. Do not add any cleaners or chemicals to your water as some are known to stain stones and others hasten erosion.

You will develop your preferences for drawing materials and surfaces as your experience – and collection – grows. Any new materials should be tested first on rocks of similar composition before using them on a gravestone. For instance, white blackboard chalk is soft and erasable whereas colored sidewalk chalks are composed of different material that scratches stones. Ink and felt-tip markers should never be used either.

Suitable paper is thin and resistant to tearing, like model-airplane tissue, acid-free museum paper, butchers' paper or shelf paper. It must also be generously larger than the design to be masking-taped tightly over the face to each side of the stone's back (other tapes may leave a sticky residue). Some taphophiles (people with a love of cemeteries) substitute heavyweight, nonfusible interface cloth for paper – it doesn't tear, is foldable and readily available in sewing shops.

Upon completing a rubbing, paper-clip your notes with the date, time and location to it – it's easy to get confused recalling one stone from the next.

Reward yourself after a day's work by adding the final touches. Spray the easily smudged rubbings with a clear acrylic fixative to set the design in place. Interface cloth is set by laying it face up on an ironing board, covering it with a tea towel and ironing it.

Once you become experienced in rubbing, you can graduate to other more advanced techniques or learn to make plaster casts.

– NIALLA NI MACHA

Dan Brown

For a superb writer, astrological clues

"A MAN on a magic carpet observes vast vistas below him." So reads the Sabian symbol for the astrological degree of author Dan Brown's natal Sun, on the Cancer-Gemini cusp. Sabian symbols are the mysterious images associated with each individual degree of the zodiac, and that gives us 360 clues to the deeper mysteries encoded in the birth chart. Sabian symbols often touch upon the essence of a birth chart's message with startling insight. They are a fitting metaphor for Dan Brown, well-known American author of the best-selling *The Da Vinci Code*, which has become a worldwide phenomenon. Witches admire Brown for his novels, which feature codes, symbols, magical keys, cryptograms and conspiracy theories. His books have sold over 80 million copies and have been translated into more than 40 languages. Regularly topping the New York Times best-seller list, works such as *Angels and Demons*, *The Lost Symbol* and *Deception Point* are among Brown's masterpieces. His thrilling plot lines usually take place within a 24-hour time frame, and often feature Robert Langdon, a protagonist in the persona of a Harvard professor.

Natal horoscope influences, early years

Dan Brown's natal horoscope can provide us with rich insight into the symbology that drives him. Brown was born just after the summer solstice on June 22, 1964. As a Cancer, history, family relationships and tradition all figure prominently in his work. His Sun conjunct North Node suggests a great scope for self-expression. In *The Da Vinci Code*, the complex interaction between Sophie Neveu and her grandfather Jacques Sauniere may have been inspired by Brown's relationship with his father. Richard Brown was an award-winning mathematics professor at the prestigious Phillips Exeter

Academy, a decidedly upscale private secondary school in New Hampshire. Brown's Cancer placements are trine his natal Saturn in Pisces, and this describes his privileged early life living at the academy. With his natal Mercury, Venus and Mars in Gemini, Dan has an alert and curious mind and an affinity for words. He flourished in the stimulating academic environment of those early years. As the oldest of three children, he often worked cryptograms and complex puzzles for hours. Each Christmas Brown's father would leave codes and clues under the tree, setting the children on a treasure hunt for gifts often secretly hidden all around the town of Exeter.

Sacred music, philosophy

Religion and music, both recurrent themes in his novels, were other influences from his childhood. His mother, Constance, was a professional musician with a special interest in sacred music. The entire family participated regularly in the church choir. After high school, Brown went on to Amherst College, where he obtained degrees in Spanish and English.

Brown's natal Moon in Sagittarius indicates his mother's influence, and indeed Brown spent several years after college pursuing a music career. He was also greatly influenced by youthful studies abroad in Spain, a Sagittarius-ruled country. His Jupiter in Taurus, a sign that has a strong association with sound, also points to his great ability and serious interest in music. Although he enjoyed some modest success as a singer and songwriter, Brown soon realized that he lacked the spark needed to become a superstar. At birth, his natal Moon was in the waxing gibbous phase, which describes a resourceful and goal-oriented person seeking purpose in life. This lunar phase is linked with the keyword "why?" Seeking knowledge adds value to life when this lunar phase is present. Brown eventually followed in his father's footsteps, returning to Phillips Exeter Academy to become a teacher.

The book on the beach

A grand cross in mutable signs involves the Gemini planets (Mercury, Venus, Mars), Uranus and Pluto in Virgo, Saturn in Pisces and the Sagittarius Moon. This union shows Brown's tremendous energy, versatility and analytical gifts. It's a chameleon-like pattern. In 1993, on vacation in Tahiti, he found a copy of Sidney Sheldon's *Doomsday Conspiracy* abandoned on the beach. Instantly Brown thought that he could write something like it. Brown attributes his entire career to that chance event.

Dan Brown is a workaholic who begins his workday at 4 a.m. An antique hourglass on his desk serves as a reminder to stop each hour for brief exercise to keep his blood flowing. He writes alone in a loft protected from distractions. Brown uses inversion therapy to overcome writer's block. He tells fans that this involves hanging upside down using anti-gravity boots. The author claims that this helps him to resolve plot challenges by providing a shift in perspective.

Success abounds

In 1995 Brown and his wife Blythe, an art historian, published a first novel together under the pseudonym Danielle Brown, *187 Men To Avoid: A Guide for the Romantically Frustrated Woman*. It is interesting to note that Dan Brown was born with Venus, the cosmic love planet, in retrograde motion. A significant age difference between marriage partners often occurs when Venus retrograde is found in the birth chart, and in fact his wife is more than a dozen years his senior. The natal Cancer influence can also indicate a preference for partners who are older or younger. The marriage has been an enduring one. In a dedication Dan thanks "Blythe Brown for her tireless research and creative input."

In 1996, Dan Brown quit teaching to become a full-time writer. He has been writing ever since. With an annual income of over 76.5 million dollars, the author has earned a place on *Forbes* Magazine's Celebrity 100 list. This great financial success can be found in his horoscope with his natal Jupiter trine Pluto in earth signs. This is supported by a wide orb grand trine in water signs involving Neptune (planet of the psychic and spiritual world), Saturn (the celestial worker) and the Sun coupled with the North Node.

Complexity-embraced, Brown's novels can take up to two years to complete. The books are magical, rich in metaphor and mystical symbolism, abounding in secret references to discover. He still revels in the spirit of the treasure hunt he enjoyed as a boy. For example, the book jacket of *The Da Vinci Code* contains hidden puzzles that provide hints about the sequel, *The Lost Symbol*. In 2001, a puzzle at the end of *Deception Point* decrypts to the message, "*The Da Vinci Code* will surface."

Brown's ideal topics present moral gray areas. They generate curiosity, debate and controversy because they don't have a clearly defined right or wrong message. A hero who is suddenly swept away from a familiar comfort zone to a strange new reality, exotic locations, dynamic women and a precarious time frame are all elements in the work. Within his books the reader encounters more than a hint of the popular axiom in witchcraft, "Within all good lies evil and within all evil lies good."

Dan Brown describes his books as "entertaining stories which promote spiritual discussion and debate." He often says that he is on "a constant spiritual journey." Glancing at the future for this enigmatic and gifted literary genius, the upcoming transit of Neptune moving into Pisces is promising. It will conjunct his Saturn in Pisces, while favorably aspecting the Sun in Cancer and Neptune in Scorpio. This creative, otherworldly and fanciful influence will be in effect from 2011 to 2025. For those who look forward to more Dan Brown novels, the future is very promising.

– DIKKI JO MULLEN

DAN BROWN

*Dan Brown was born on June 22, 1964
in Exeter, New Hampshire.*

42 N 58'53" 70 W 55'54" A noon-style chart is used
as the exact birth time is unknown

Data Table
(Tropical Placidus Houses and Ascendant at Noon)

Sun 1 Cancer 14 – 10th house

Moon 5 Sagittarius 23 – 3rd house (Gibbous Moon Phase)

Mercury 25 Gemini 32 – 10th house

Venus 26 Gemini 56 – 10th house (retrograde)

Mars 3 Gemini 41 – 9th house

Jupiter 16 Taurus 20–- 8th house

Saturn 5 Pisces 00 – 6th house (retrograde)

Uranus 6 Virgo 37 – 12th house

Neptune 15 Scorpio 22 – 2nd house (retrograde)

Pluto 11 Virgo 50 – 12th house

Chiron 18 Pisces 48 – 6th house (retrograde)

N. Moon Node 2 Cancer 05

Ascendant or Rising Sign is 22 Virgo 10

More Keys of Solomon

PEOPLE WHO know the history of magic just from books may be excused for thinking that there are only two grimoires called *The Key of Solomon* (the King of Israel), for there were only two of them that could be found in the bookstores until quite recently. One was usually called *The Greater Key of Solomon*. It was edited by S.L. MacGregor Mathers from seven manuscripts in the British Library, and it was first published in 1889. The other was sometimes called *The Lesser Key of Solomon*, sometimes *The Book of the Goetia*. It, too, had been edited by Mathers from a very few manuscripts, but it was first published by Aleister Crowley in 1904.

Yet this is not the whole story. If you look through the old manuscripts 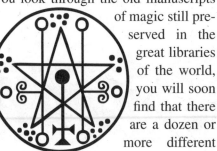 of magic still preserved in the great libraries of the world, you will soon find that there are a dozen or more different *Keys of Solomon*. To be sure, a few of them have been given new, far more mysterious titles, but even so they are easily recognized as variants or derivatives of works called *Keys of Solomon*.

Often, too, fanciful histories have been made up and placed at the front of these grimoires: one of them was, so it is claimed, translated by 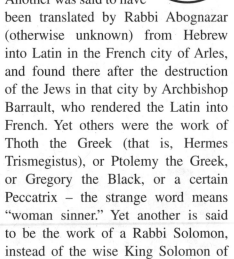 the illustrious Jewish scholar Abraham Colorno at the command of a Duke of Mantua. Another was said to have been translated by Rabbi Abognazar (otherwise unknown) from Hebrew into Latin in the French city of Arles, and found there after the destruction of the Jews in that city by Archbishop Barrault, who rendered the Latin into French. Yet others were the work of Thoth the Greek (that is, Hermes Trismegistus), or Ptolemy the Greek, or Gregory the Black, or a certain Peccatrix – the strange word means "woman sinner." Yet another is said to be the work of a Rabbi Solomon, instead of the wise King Solomon of

Israel. (This one is a particularly well-organized and interesting grimoire.) — And so forth. You should keep many grains of salt close at hand as you try to swallow these stories.

A new book has just appeared, edited by the well-known magicians Stephen Skinner and David Rankine, which contains two of these unknown Solomonic grimoires in new English translations, as well as a new translation of the so-called *Greater Key*, made from a manuscript that Mathers did not use. The book's title is *The Veritable Key of Solomon*, and it was published in several editions. The hitherto unpublished grimoires that it offers the magically-minded reader are "The Keys of Rabbi Solomon" and the "Universal Treatise of the Keys of Solomon." It also contains a substantial preface and appendices, which build on 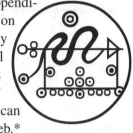 an earlier study of mine of all the various forms of the *Key of Solomon*, which can be read on the web.*

– ROBERT MATHIESEN

*"The Key of Solomon: Toward a Typology of the Manuscripts," *Societas Magica Newsletter* 17 (Spring 2007), on the Society's website at <www.societasmagica.org>.

Kings bringing gifts to Solomon

The Golem
From dust, to dust

HASHEM created the world through speech. Hashem said, "Let there be light," and it was so. He said, "Let there be day and night; Let the waters be divided; Let the water and land and sky fill with creatures," and all was so. As He spoke these divine commands He cast the letters of the Hebrew alphabet – from Aleph through Tev – down to earth. And as they fell they combined, forming all the creatures that now roam the Earth. Aleph, Reish, and Yod combined to form Aree, the Lion; Shin and Hei combined to form Sah, the lamb. And once all the letters had fallen, and combined, and yielded great varieties of creature, Hashem looked upon creation and saw that it was good. But His creation was still incomplete. And so Hashem molded His final creature in His own image from the clay of the

newly formed Earth. With the letters Aleph, Dalet, and Samekh Hashem created Adam, the Human.

According to the Torah, Adam is the only of Hashem's creations to posses an eternal soul and thus the ability to use and understand language, which comes directly from Hashem. However, for the first twelve hours of Adam's existence he had no soul: he was a mute, shapeless hunk of clay. Before Hashem spoke and granted Adam a soul Adam was not a human but a Golem.

The Golem (GOH-lem) is a mythological creature forged from clay and brought to life by only the most spiritually dedicated of rabbis. A Golem, while physically resembling a human, is slow moving, slow witted, unable to think or act on its own, and cannot speak. The word Golem is derived from "Gelem" or "raw material" and is also related to "Goylem" or "unshaped form" and "Ghulam" or "servant." Golem translates literally to "cocoon," implying the Golem to be a shell rather than a complete being. Indeed, since a Golem's life comes from a man and not directly from Hashem, a Golem has no soul.

The Kabbalistic book of formation, the *Sefer Hayetzera*, contains directions on making a Golem. First, clay is shaped into the rough form of a man, just as Hashem shaped Adam from the Earth. Next, the rough form is placed on the ground and the creator dances around it in a circle, reciting the four letters, which represent the secret name of Hashem. Alternatively, the four letters can be written on parchment and placed in the Golem's mouth, or the letters Aleph, Mem, and Tav, spelling Emet or "Truth" can be carved on the Golem's forehead. Whichever method is used, the proper application of language is the crucial component in raising a Golem.

Once brought to life the Golem is completely obedient to its creator, but a Golem can only be created by those devoted enough to have knowledge of the secret name of Hashem – and only for a serious purpose. Usually, a Golem is called upon to protect a Jewish community in a time of crisis. One well-known story takes place in Prague during a pogrom. In the late sixteenth century a blood libel – an accusation of the ritual murder of Christian children – was brought against the Jewish community in Prague. In response, Rudolph II, Holy Roman Emperor, ordered all the Jews in Prague either expelled or killed. Concerned for the safety of his community, the Rabbi Loew, also known as the Maharal of Prague, conjured a Golem on the banks of the Vltava River. The Golem, twice as tall and twice as wide as any man, was ordered to protect the Jews from harm. The Golem wandered the streets of Prague, dispersing angry crowds and killing anyone who tried to bring harm

to any Jew, inspiring fear wherever he brought his massive, unnatural form. After several days of the Golem's reign of terror, Rudolph II approached Rabbi Loew and begged him to call the Golem back. And so a deal was struck between the two leaders: the Rabbi would call off the Golem and Rudolph II would end his pogrom against the Jews.

No one can say for sure what happened to the Golem of Prague after the deal between Rudolph II and Rabbi Loew was struck. Some accounts say Rabbi Loew stored the Golem in the attic of the old synagogue, ready to be brought back in case of future threats. In fact, it is rumored the old synagogue escaped destruction during Nazi occupation because the Golem was protecting it. Others say Rabbi Loew started using the Golem to perform menial household chores, with unfortunate consequences: one day the Rabbi told the Golem to fetch water from the well. Feeling tired, the Rabbi then retired to

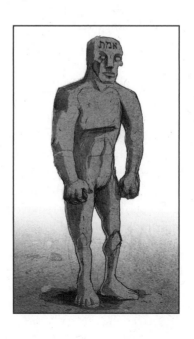

his room for a nap. When he awoke an hour later, the house was flooding with water! The Golem had been fetching water, as instructed, but did not have the reasoning faculties to stop when the task was done. This left the Rabbi with no choice but to destroy the Golem.

There are several reasons to destroy a Golem. For one, if his noble task has been completed and the community has been defended, there is no righteous purpose to keep the Golem alive. If a Golem remains alive for longer than it is needed, it tends to become willful, disobedient, and very often will turn on its creator. Golems also tend to grow larger and larger the longer they live. A giant, willful Golem is a danger to everyone.

Just as language brings a Golem to life, language is also employed when destroying a Golem. One can walk backwards around the Golem while reciting the four letters of the secret name of Hashem, or the parchment containing these letters can be removed from the Golem's mouth. If "Emet" has been written on the Golem's forehead, the Aleph can be removed, leaving the word "Met." Thus, "Truth" becomes "Death" and the Golem is destroyed. One Golem legend tells of a Golem who grew so big its creator knew it must be destroyed before it hurt anyone. So the Rabbi asked the Golem to tie his shoe. When the Golem bent down to follow his order, the Rabbi removed the Aleph from the Golem's forehead. The Golem immediately turned back into inanimate clay. Unfortunately, the great mass of clay fell forward and crushed the Rabbi, killing him instantly.

The Golem, though ancient in origin, still makes his presence felt today. A statue of the legendary hero stands at the entrance of the old Jewish quarter in Prague. Prague is also home to a Golem Museum. The Golem has appeared in many novels, poetry, and plays of the twentieth century. America's modern superheroes are strongly influenced by the Golem legend – notions not at all surprising considering many of the forefathers of the medium were practicing Jews. The Golem is also the inspiration for our modern conception of Robots – man made automatons designed to follow our orders. The word Robot, derived from the Czech word "robata" or work, was first used in Karel Capek's 1923 play, "Rossum's Universal Robots," a text that borrows heavily from the original Golem legend. In more recent history, the G.O.L.E.M. project – Genetically Organized Lifelike Electro Mechanics – exploits a computer program that allows robots to actually design and build themselves – the first time ever a robot has actually participated in its own creation.

According to Hebrew lore, from the creation of the first human to the creation of the first self-realizing robot, the Golem has always been with us – a constant reminder of what we really are – inanimate matter turned animate through the Miracle of Language.

– SHANNON MARKS

Gobekli Tepe

A new concept of human origins

A DISCOVERY IN Turkey has exploded in archaeological circles. Attention is riveted on Gobekli Tepe, a site not far from the plains of Harran, Syria, and the ancient lands of Mesopotamia. Below the surface of "potbelly hill" lies a huge, beautiful temple complex, its size and age wildly predating all other evidence of human ascent. The structure originated 11,500 years ago – 7,000 years before the Great Pyramid, more than 6,000 years before Stonehenge. To get a further handle on the mind-boggling numbers, the unique ruins preceded village communities, domestic animals, pottery and agriculture.

Klaus Schmidt, a German archaeologist, has turned up an extraordinary network of carved stone circles. Each features monumental T-shaped pillars evoking the gigantic heads crumbling on Easter Island. In addition to the 50 pillars uncovered, radar indicates another 15 or 20 more such circles await digging. According to carbon dating, these are the oldest monumental artworks in the world.

Schmidt believes that Gobekli Tepe constituted "the Rome of the Ice Age," where surviving hunter-gatherers met to worship and build a temple complex. Once assembled, they needed a staple source of food. Inhabitants made the transformation into farming – the giant step of mankind's ascent. The site implies that creating gods created agriculture, tossing accepted theory upside-down.

Merry Meetings

*A candle in the window, a fire on the hearth,
a discourse over tea…*

This year we had an opportunity to speak with Michael 'Mike' Howard, an English witch and magus. The author of over thirty books, he has been actively involved in the craft and magical traditions for over forty-five years. He is the editor and publisher of *The Cauldron*, a respected magazine in the field of witchcraft, magic, and folklore, published continuously since 1976, enjoying a world-wide readership.

Our staff enjoys your magazine very much and considers it an essential resource for those with a personal interest in witchcraft and the magical arts. What sort of life experiences or influences were at work to spark your initial interest in these disciplines?

I became interested in the occult and the supernatural in my early teens through reading fictional works by authors such as Algernon Blackwood, Arthur Machen, Dennis Wheatley, M.R. James, and H.P. Lovecraft. Then in 1963, I read a newspaper report about the discovery of evidence of a so-called black magic rite at a ruined church in an English village. A skeleton had been removed from a grave and used in what looked to be a necromantic rite. I then realized that people were still carrying out occult practices and it was for real.

My first real encounter with witchcraft in this life was when I was studying at agricultural college in rural Somerset. I met an old countryman who told me of female witches he knew who could cure and curse and a local wise-man skilled in "owl blasting."

This was a dialect term for casting the evil eye. When I graduated from the college I went to work on a farm in Gloucestershire. There I was lucky enough to meet an old-style witch or cunning man. He convinced me that witchcraft of a traditional or historical form was still being practised in the English countryside.

You have written about being involved with Madeline Montalban and her magical group, the Order of the Morning Star. In The Pillars of Tubal Cain *you indicate that her teachings regarding the biblical fallen angels or Watchers, are integral to understanding the importance of witchcraft as it has developed in Western culture. Could you give us an overview of the importance of the magical system used by the OMS and what our readers should seek to learn about the Watchers and Lumiel-Lucifer? Also, how did your work with Madeline Montalban affect your own personal path?*

I met Madeline Montalban in the famous hippy "summer of love" in 1967. Madeline was not a witch, although there are persistent rumors she was associated or involved with traditional witchcraft before the war. She was a magician, taromancer, and astrologer who wrote monthly horoscopes and articles for a popular astrological magazine called *Prediction*. She produced a practical course that taught her students angelic magic based on medieval grimoires such as *The Key of Solomon*, Agrippa's *Occult Philosophy* and Francis Barrett's *The Magus*. However, when they reached a certain point in the course, students then were introduced to the "big secret"– the teachings about the fallen angels and their leader Azazel, also known as the rebel archangel Lucifer or Lumiel the Lightbearer. If they did not run off screaming, they could then progress further.

The OMS was important because it was one of the first modern occult groups to present Luciferianism in a non-satanic, gnostic way and as a legitimate part of the Western magical tradition. It represented Lord Lumiel and the Fallen Ones in a positive way as cultural exemplars and teachers and guides to humanity, rather than the evil spirits of biblical propaganda. After I left the Order I still remained dedicated in secret to Lord Lumiel and the Luciferian tradition. It was only in the 1990s that I decided to go public on that aspect of my occult life. Basically I think that those Witches' Almanac readers who feel sincerely attracted to the Luciferian tradition should attempt to make their own personal contact with the Lightbearer and his Watchers or "Teaching Angels." They will find the Fallen Ones will answer the call of any sincere seeker wishing to learn.

You have an impressive catalog of over thirty books. What motivated you to start writing? Do you have a background in journalism, or was it a case of the spirit moving you to share your personal discoveries and knowledge?

Writing is in my blood as I have also been interested in expressing my thoughts using that medium since my school days. When I met Madeline Montalban, she encouraged me to do it professionally and helped me get my first article published in *Prediction* in 1970. In fact, I wrote articles and book reviews for *Prediction* for over twenty years. She was a trained journalist and had worked before the Second World War for a national newspaper and an international press agency, so she was a good teacher for an aspiring writer.

I got a publishing contract for my first book, on candle magic, because the Cabbalistic magician W.E. Butler mentioned me to the now defunct Aquarian Press. They had asked Ernest to write a book on the subject, but he declined as he believed he did not have the "popular touch." Instead he suggested they ask me. Then I managed to get a recommendation from Nigel Pennick so that Thorsons Publishers commissioned me to write my first of several books on the Northern European runes.

To be honest I never really started out to write as a teaching tool or to impart knowledge. That was something that developed and became a more important and primary reason for my writings. The initial motive was so I could give up mundane work and devote myself to it as a career. It soon became apparent that it was impossible to make a living out of writing serious esoteric books. My conscience would not allow me to write populist garbage that would sell and I was totally hopeless at fiction, where good money can be earned if you are good at it.

In 1976 you founded The Cauldron. *How has this venture served your own spiritual journey and the larger effort to enhance the journeys of readers? Can you name a few of the writers published in the magazine who have made an exceptional contribution to the field?*

Publishing *The Cauldron* for the last thirty-six years has been a magical labor of love and a service for the craft. It is non-profit making and I have never tried or wanted to make any money out of it. Today its back issues are widely sought after as collector's items. They are also regarded by those academics studying ancient and modern witchcraft as an important and valuable historical resource. Over the years, it has flown the banner of traditional craft high by publishing articles by contemporary writers in that field like Nigel Aldcroft Jackson, E.W. Liddell, Martin Duffy, Nigel Pennick, Evan John Jones, Shani Oates, Alaister Clay-Egerton, Andrew D. Chumbley, and Daniel A. Schulke. My own personal journey on the path has been enhanced by editing and publishing *The Cauldron* because of the number of contacts in traditional craft I have made through it and the good people I have encountered. Some of these became friends and also fellow companions on the path.

In 2000 you authored Light From the Shadows: A Mythos of Modern Traditional Witchcraft *under the pen-name Gwyn. This book delves into the lore and esoteric spirituality of traditional craft, rather than the nuts and bolts of spellcraft and sorcery. How do these two distinct areas of magical praxis mesh in the modern manifestation of traditional witchcraft?*

Before answering your last question, I would like to digress into the raison d'être for writing *Light From the Shadows* and why I did not put my real name to it. Since my initiation into Gardnerian Wicca, I had not felt comfortable about and wary of writing books on the craft because of its naturally secretive nature. That is why when I wrote *Light From the Shadows* I used a pen-name. The book was written as guide to newbies and beginners, but it did not turn out exactly how I wanted it to. I felt pressured to sanitize and popularize the subject for the publisher. However, people seemed to have liked it anyway and found it informative and helpful. As a result, since its publication

I have changed my views and will be writing more books on the craft.

The magical practices in modern traditional witchcraft deal with charms, spells, shapechanging, necromancy, astral travel, trance work, exorcism, wortcunning or "green magic" involving herbal and plant lore, healing and cursing, communing with the spirit world, and divination. The so-called religious or spiritual aspects include celebrating the Witches' Sabbath, observing seasonal customs where it is appropriate or needful, and sacrifice, reverence and devotion to the ancestral dead, spirits, angels, and deities.

My own personal view is that the craft is a gnostic magico-spiritual mystery cultus. Its goal is spiritual enlightenment and illumination and the control of the practitioner's own karmic destiny. This is also the end-game of so-called high magic or theurgy in the Western mystery tradition. The practical magical dimension or context to witchcraft is represented by so-called low magic, folk magic or sorcery. The sorcerer is someone, male or female, who is willing to make a pact with the spirits in exchange for magical power and occult knowledge and then wield and use that power in the material world.

You are currently embarked on some new projects for future books. What can we look forward to in the coming years?

In recent years my writing has gone through a very productive stage. This is not unconnected with my magical practice and involvement with the Cultus Sabbati and its members. As a result I have several books recently published, awaiting publication, or in the pipeline, and some future writing projects that are still in my head.

I have been working for the new esoteric publishing company, Three Hands Press, in the USA on a series of books about historical witches and cunning folk in regions of the British Isles. They are also going to publish my book on traditional witchcraft. I've also had a history of modern wicca published recently by Llewellyn.

At present my focus is on the American market because it has a larger potential readership base than the UK. I am therefore hoping that my books can get a wider audience in the future. It is very difficult now to get serious books on witchcraft and magic accepted here by mainstream publishing houses as they are concentrating on new age titles. I am particularly happy that my book on traditional witchcraft has an American publisher. This is because there is a growing interest in the subject in the US and also a lot of misconceptions and misinformation over there about the subject. Hopefully my book will help to counteract that.

A complete bibliography and contact information along with further excerpts from this interview may be found at http://TheWitchesAlmanac.com/AlmanacExtras/.

DIA DE LOS MUERTOS

Feasting to honor ancestors

HALLOWEEN HAS been usurped, turned into today's constant carnival of Goths and vampires, with zombie movies and games of the supernatural everywhere. This is a crime against children, whose magic holiday it once was, and I am paying little or no attention to it now. Instead, I'm moving toward another celebration: Dia de Los Muertos, or Day of the Dead, Mexico's loving tribute to those from the other side of the grave.

A superficial glance at the images representing it reveals dancing skeletons and rattling bones, bizarre sugar candy skulls and brightly colored tissue paper scissored into death themed panels. These handicrafts are parts of the tradition – but only the most obvious, more commercial ones. A deeper look finds countless ways of honoring the dead with food and drink, flowers and artifacts, incense and candles, music and dance. While the occasion is a serious combination of indigenous memories and Roman Catholicism, it is also whimsical and joyous, with playful festivities leading up to its celebration between October 31 and November 2.

Throughout Mexico there are regional variations in customs. To invite the return of the spirits of those who have gone before, altars (*ofrendas*) are created in homes: tables covered in bright cloth (sometimes with lacy green stalks of sugar cane tied to the legs and arched over the surface) laden with foods, drink, favorite possessions – cigarettes, new clothing, toys for children, photographs. Candles burn day and night; the distinctive smell of copal (a resin used as incense) fills the air. In Patzcuaro, decorated boats ferry people across the largest lake to island cemeteries where they spend the night among candlelit graves; Oaxacans bearing gifts and flowers visit outlying villages famous for artistic altars; Mexico City's museums and public spaces stage exhibits of altars along with music and dance.

To prepare for the feast that is served to both the living and the dead, women gather for days, making piles of slow steamed tamales, both sweet and savory. They bake ceremonial breads – large coffeecake-like sweet breads decorated with "bones" of cut-out dough and small rolls (some in fanciful animal shapes for children who have died). From the recent harvest they create dishes from pumpkin, beans and corn, and nourishing *atole*, thick drinks of corn *masa* mixed with pineapple or other fruits. Hot chocolate is comforting in cool evenings, made with spiced chocolate discs, mixed into milk by twirling a wooden *molinillo*. Huge pots of meaty stews and hearty soups are prepared to offset the effects of mescal and tequila consumed during the reunions of families and friends. Flowers are gathered in profusion; most popular are marigolds, their pungent scent believed to attract wandering spirits to their homes.

By November 3 all returns to normal. The dead have been honored, the living go on to face the change of the season with shorter days and longer nights, a darker time of year.

Bread is one of the most important items on every altar. *Pan de Muertos* – Day of the Dead Bread – is baked in abundance for presentation and to be shared with guests. The recipe that follows is baked as a round loaf that may be adorned with crossed "bones" made from some of the dough, placed around the knob on top.

Pan de Muertos

1/4 cup each butter, milk and
   warm water (110 degrees)
3 cups all-purpose flour
1 1/4 teaspoons active dry yeast
1/2 teaspoon salt
2 teaspoons anise seed
1/4 cup white sugar
2 eggs, beaten
2 teaspoons orange zest

Glaze

1/4 cup white sugar
1/4 cup orange juice
1 tablespoon orange zest
2 tablespoons white sugar

Heat the milk and butter together in a medium saucepan until the butter melts. Remove from heat and add warm water. The mixture should be around 110 degrees.

In a large bowl combine 1 cup of flour, yeast, salt, anise seed and 1/4 cup of sugar. Beat in the warm milk mixture, then add the eggs and two teaspons orange zest and beat until well combined. Stir in 1/2 cup of flour and continue adding more flour until the dough is soft.

Turn the dough out onto a lightly floured surface and knead until smooth and elastic.

Place the dough in a lightly greased bowl, cover with plastic wrap and let rise in a warm place until doubled in size (about 1-2 hours). Punch the dough down and shape it into a large round loaf with a round knob on top. Place on a baking sheet, loosely covered with plastic wrap, and let rise in a warm place for about 1 hour or until just about doubled in size.

Bake in a preheated 350 degree oven for about 35-45 minutes. Remove from oven and let cool slightly.

Meanwhile, make the glaze: In a small saucepan combine the 1/4 cup sugar, orange juice and one tablespoon orange zest. Bring to a boil over medium heat and boil for 2 minutes. Brush over top of bread while still warm. Sprinkle glazed bread with white sugar.

Pumpkin is used in many ways for feasting during Dia de los Muertos. It is included in stews and soups, made into a filling for tamales, its seeds are hulled and eaten as sugar glazed or salted snacks (*pepitas*). One of the favorite dishes is a long-cooked sweet made with *piloncillo* (a dark brown form of sugar sold in solid cones), eaten warm for breakfast with cream, or as dessert, chilled and paired with vanilla ice cream. The version that follows is loosely based on a recipe from Michoacan and it uses regular brown sugar – a lot of it.

Calabaza en Tacha
1 medium pumpkin, about 5 pounds
(sugar pumpkin preferred)
8 cups water, approximately
1 1/2 pounds (about 4 cups)
   dark brown sugar
2 cinnamon sticks (3-4 inches each)

Keep rind on to prevent skin from falling apart during cooking. Wash and dry pumpkin. Poke holes with a knife in several spots to allow syrup to penetrate flesh.

Cut pumpkin in half lengthwise, clean out seeds and fibers, then cut it into 3-inch chunks or crescent slices.

In a wide heavy pot (Dutch oven) add pumpkin, sugar and cinnamon sticks. Add enough water to cover completely.

Bring to a boil. Cover pot and cook pumpkin over medium high heat 15 minutes. Remove lid. Simmer, uncovered, until liquid is reduced to thick syrup and pumpkin is tender and glazed, 1-2 hours.

Julian Medina is chef of Toloache, a noted Mexican restaurant in Manhattan. He created the following recipe to be served as part of a Day of the Dead menu several years ago.

Candied Pumpkin Seeds
1 pound hulled pumpkin seeds (*pepitas*:
   look for them in bulk foods sections)
1 cup granulated sugar
White of one large egg
1/2 teaspoon ground cinnamon

Heat oven to 300 degrees. Combine all ingredients in large mixing bowl, stirring well to thoroughly combine. Spread mixture evenly in a rimmed baking sheet.

Bake for 30 minutes, stirring every 5 minutes. Remove baking sheet from oven and place on a rack to cool.

– Pat Fusco

Reprinted from PacificSun.

A Magical Leap, 2012

February 29, rarest of days

"KEEP TIME with a leap now and then" advised another almanac nearly two centuries ago. The line derives from the 1820 Leap Year Edition of *The Farmer's Almanac*, marking the occasion with humor, poetry and art. We celebrate the rarest of days, February 29, again in our time, 2012. In addition, the Mayan Calendar and other sources predict this year will be an important turning point.

It seems appropriate that we encounter Leap Day at the end of Valentine's month. According to what the tradition brings to certain couples, some hearts will rise and others will sink, confused and disoriented. Perhaps you haven't noticed the event in your calendar and datebook; many electronic calendars and perpetual datebooks totally miss the date between February 28 and March 1, further complicating the issue. Some of us might arrive for an appointment a day early. Workers who are scrambling to meet a March 1st deadline can suddenly be gifted with an extra day. The twenty-four-hour grace period can be used to tie up loose ends or just to rest and procrastinate before the onset of the new month.

Few birthday parties

Of all the delights and frustrations the 29th of February can bring, perhaps the souls born on that day experience the most extreme feelings – they have the most infrequent of birthdays. Perhaps that's why these people often follow a mystical, nonconformist life path. Mother Ann Lee, who founded the Shakers, was a leaper or leapling, as leap year babies are called, but so was Aileen Wuornos, Florida's and notorious serial killer. Leapers must cherish each birthday, remembering that "less is more," for they can only celebrate once every four years. Occasionally some are inclined to borrow February 28 or March 1 as a birthday.

The fixed star Skaat in Pisces is close enough to impact Leap Day astrologically. A 4th magnitude star in the leg of the Water Bearer, its keywords are intuitive, nervous, visionary and illusionary. In the first decanate of Pisces, this shows a double Neptune, a strong water rulership.

The Sabian symbol for Leap Day is "an aviator in the clouds," the keyword is observation and brings the gift of higher perspective. An exploratory and otherworldly quality is present. In the Tarot the High Priestess links to Leap Day, further indicating depth, mysterious wisdom and hidden messages.

To keep the calendar in synch an entire day every four years is just a bit too much, so occasionally Leap Year is skipped. In 1700, 1800 and 1900 no Leap Days were added to the calendar in order to keep the record straight. However in 2000, the 29th of February appeared again. Leap Day is unique, it just can't be anything other than an extraordinary day.

Romantic traditions

In antique shops you can sometimes find vintage postcards from the early twentieth century greeting Leap Days, and one composer wrote a Leap Year Waltz. *Leap Year*, a popular film starring Amy Adams, was released in 2010. Set in Ireland, the plot revolved around the longtime custom of celebrating Leap Day as Bachelor's Day. It was the only time a lady could properly propose marriage to a gentleman. In earlier times singles of either gender considered it a fortunate day to agree to a proposal. But if a bachelor did want to refuse, he had to present the rejected lady with a new silk dress to get off the hook.

Plan to savor and celebrate this Leap Day. An intercalculatory calendar day, it was gifted to the mini month of February. Do you welcome the day or tend to trip over it? Either way, it's there for your choosing.

Calculation nightmare

With all this hassle, can't we skip Leap Day? Absolutely not. Except for the Chinese Calendar and a few alternatives such as the Hebrew Calendar or Native American Medicine Wheels, the calendar used by most of the world today is solar based, oriented toward Earth's trek around the Sun. But a glitch occurs. We have a tidy 365-day calendar, but the Earth's orbital time is actually 365 days, 5 hours, 48 minutes and 45.51 seconds. Almost six hours over four years add up to nearly a whole day needed to stay in synch with the solar system.

The road to this realization has been a surprisingly bumpy one. The arrangement of days that make up our familiar and beloved calendars came about after centuries of valiant and off-target attempts to keep track of time. The ancient Egyptians managed with twelve months of thirty days followed by five feast days, a vacation at the end of the year when everyone celebrated. By 238 BCE, in the time of Ptolemy III, it became obvious that an extra feast day would have to be added every fourth year. This change wasn't acceptable, since the Egyptians worked according to the agricultural seasons. If the calendar wasn't adjusted, it could indicate midsummer when a freeze might arrive. In the eighth century BCE, Romulus, the first King of Rome, devised a system of ten lunar months. Since the Moon's cycle isn't consistent, the ten-month calendar would need even more feasting time to keep up.

Another Roman, Numa Pompilus, shortened some months and used the leftover days to create January and

February. This year was too short, so he added an intercalendary twenty-seven-day cycle called Mercedonious. This leap month was supposed to be added in alternate years. However, the criminal minds of the officials in charge of things misused the system. They extended terms of political office or changed debt collection dates, among other sleazy activities, until eventually Mercedonius just vanished.

When Julius Caesar came to power in 47 BCE, the calendar indicated January but Mother Nature indicated autumn harvest season. Caesar did a really bright thing; he called in a top-notch astrologer for help. A ninety-day fix was added and ever since, 46 BCE has been called The Year of Confusion, with its 445 days. However, the calendar was back in tune with the seasons. The next year a neat 365-day calendar with a Leap Day added every fourth year was implemented – the famous Julian Calendar.

For a long time this seemed fine. But do you remember that extra 1/4 or so day? By 1582 it added up to fifteen days and the seasons were getting askew again. A great Italian astrologer, Aloysius Lilius, came to the rescue. He designed a new calendar, the one we use today. Since this happened when

Pope Gregory arose to power, it was named the Gregorian calendar. We call it the New Style Calendar and it is the one we use today. The Julian Calendar is the Old Style Calendar, although it was still used in places through the early twentieth century.

To keep the calendar accurate, every time the year ends in 00 we skip Leap Year. That's unless the 00 year is divisible by 4 with no remainder. That's why 2000 was a Leap Year, but 1900 wasn't. So why is this called Leap Year? That's another story. In a normal year, the day of the week aligned with a date moves forward one day each year. If your birthday was on Tuesday this year, it will be on Wednesday next year. That is unless it's Leap Year; then the spare day moves forward or leaps the weekly sequence ahead.

Leap Day is now becoming a popular modern holiday. Don't let it fall into a chasm, smile at its checkered past and celebrate with good humor. Most February 29 babies do. They can take any time they please for a birthday celebration, except during the rare years when the gift of the extra day rolls around.

– Dikki Jo Mullen

More Leap Year information is available on line at http://TheWitches Almanac.com/AlmanacExtras/.

Hobos, Tramps and Bums

A glimpse into Hobohemia

SUPREME COURT justice William O. Douglas, actor and folk singer Burl Ives, novelists Jack London and Ernest Hemingway, British poet W.H. Davis, as well as television personality Art Linkletter all went through phases of "being homesick for their freedom," as the "knights of the road" were wont to explain. As young men, all of them rode the rails for travel and adventure, just a few of the notables who at one time lived as hobos.

The origin of the word hobo, first coined in the late 19th century, is uncertain. Some linguists say it came from hoe-boy, signifying a migratory farm laborer. Others cite the Latin words *homo bonus* which translates as "good man." Other sources say it's an abbreviation for *ho*meward *bo*und.

During an eighty year period, from shortly after the Civil War, through the Great Depression and World War II, penniless wanderers, usually young men, took to hopping on freight trains. When times became hard, their ranks swelled and were thought to make up 0.05% of the U.S. population, numbering perhaps 700,000 souls. Some were trying to find their way home, others were looking for work. Still others were seeking better luck while following some personal and private dream. These vagabonds, variously called hobos, tramps and bums, were often lumped together by those living a more settled and conventional life yet among their own ranks the contrast is considered great.

Gentlemen of the Road versus Lazy Bums

A hobo traveled in order to work, skillfully earning "three hots and a cot" while pursuing a life free of responsibilities and roots. Many hobos looked upon the lifestyle as an extended adventure before returning to school, a profession or family ties. Hobos considered themselves gentlemen of the road. A tramp was often snobbish, a brilliant intellectual who traveled extensively, preferring to live by his wits, unless compelled to work. Tramps and hobos would travel to see, observe, and experience life. A bum ranked the lowest of the trio. "Lazy bums," usually alcoholics, would seek hand outs and only move or work when forced to by the police. Living spontaneously, choosing freedom, and escaping civilization's rut while being road worthy and self reliant is at the core of hobo and tramp philosophy, although not the bum's.

"Mov'in on" was always a dangerous lifestyle. Nevertheless, like a steam engine building momentum, many heeded the call. When rules were too hard to follow; a dream made conformity undesirable; or deep disappointment struck; a certain type of man would be drawn to pursue new horizons and adventure. Survival depended on developing the skill of riding under, on or in railroad freight cars. Railroad security officers called "bulls" would often beat or even kill any vagabonds they could catch.

Celebrating Hobohemia

For over a century, the small farming town of Britt, Iowa has been the kindest, most accommodating place for the often misunderstood and abused hobos to congregate safely. A "jungle," the term for a hobo camp, is established in Britt as is a permanent museum of hobo art, writings and photographs. On August 22, 1900, the first annual Hobo Convention was held in Britt. Former and current hobos from all over continue to gather each August for a couple of weeks alongside aficionados of hobo culture to enjoy the company of those who share their transient path, exchange stories and celebrate the ramblin' life. Then they feel the call to move on.

The King and Queen of Hobos

During the convention, a King of Hobos is elected and, since 1946, a Queen. Former Kings and Queens describe relishing the experience. They appreciated being treated like royalty, at least for a day.

Traditionally, an important component of hobo identity involves adopting a new name especially for use on the road. The famous names of hobo royalty include: Cannonball Eddie, Slow Motion Shorty, Highway Johnny, Steam Train Maury, Scoop Shovel Scotty, Pennsylvania Kid, Grandpa Dudley, Inkman and the recently elected Tuck. Polly Ellen Pep was the first Hobo Queen, a title she held for at least three years, until Box Car Myrtle was crowned, followed by lovelies named Mama Jo, Cinderbox Cindy and Minneapolis Jewel.

Hobos Today

Yes, this unique style of life still exists today, although probably fewer than 500 true hobos remain. Even the mayor of Britt discourages riding the rails of modern trains. It's far too dangerous, not to say illegal. Many convention-goers now arrive in campers or on motorcycles. However, some new wanderers are joining the ranks of the older retired hobos and keeping their traditions alive.

Stray Cat, among the younger hobos, became Queen in 2009 and has been hopping trains for at least nine years without any definite plans or destination in mind. Stretch is another who has been "mov'in on" for over twenty five years. There are also numerous "friends of hobos," those dedicated to preserving hobo culture.

Hobo Art

Traditional hobo art forms include the intricate whittling of a single piece of wood to fashion linked chains, balls in a cage, or bottles filled with miniature carvings as well as paintings, music, storytelling, poetry, and etched coins. The coins, usually buffalo nickels, are highly collectible numismatics now, often selling for hundreds of dollars. The hobo artist would painstakingly work the metal until the original design became an Indian Chief, clown, bird, four leaf lucky clover, skull, model train, Roman Emperor or other creative vision. Now valued as art, originally hobo creations were bartered for food and lodging.

Hobo Adman, an otherwise respectable professional man and home owner is known as Todd Waters for most of the year. Adman's wife understands his occasional need for freedom. When the rails get warm and are rich with the smell of creosote each spring, she knows Adman must answer the call. Adman recently took his 20 year old daughter Alex along on a journey.

During a conversation at the Britt, Iowa annual hobo convention, Alex reflected that "she never knew what sleeping in the woods without a cell phone, or tent would actually feel like." Whether following it is your own cup of "Mulligan Stew" – a hobo meal made in a single pot over a campfire – or not, the witch can certainly appreciate the compelling magic of the Hobo Code. It really means to decide your own life.

– MARINA BRYONY

A glossary of some of the terms used in hobo conversations may be found at http://TheWitchesAlmanac.com/AlmanacExtras/.

The Secret Language

ALTHOUGH some citizens were helpful and quite friendly, others were hostile, so hobos developed a series of marks, usually drawn with chalk. Before they had to get moving, as they really couldn't stay put, many hobos would leave a kind of travel journal. This secret vocabulary went unnoticed by the uninitiated, but would tell those in the know what to expect at each stop.

Here are some of the most well known hobo markings:

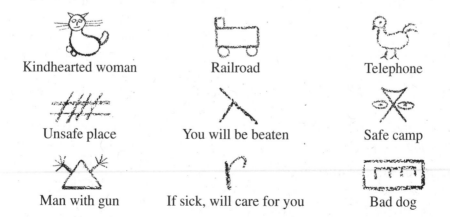

Kindhearted woman	Railroad	Telephone
Unsafe place	You will be beaten	Safe camp
Man with gun	If sick, will care for you	Bad dog

An Apple a Day

Uttwiler Spatlauber

GROWING in a lonely and remote part of Switzerland, the Uttwiler Spatlauber is a mysterious and rare apple. Although tiny, tart and unremarkable, these apples were widely cultivated as a source of emergency food during the 18th century. Each tree is very prolific but more significantly, apples produced remain fresh, lasting many months longer than sweeter and tastier fruits. In the days before refrigeration and other methods of food preservation were available, these Swiss apples were treasured and appreciated. However, as the years passed and society evolved, they were neglected, nearly forgotten and eventually almost extinct. Only three trees remained by the year 2000.

Then, like an enchanted heroine from a fairy tale, their unexpected magic was unveiled. Someone wondered what kept these particular apples alive for so long. Furthermore, it was observed that if the tree's bark or fruit was cut or bruised, it would quickly heal. The cells produced throughout the life of the tree, both for growth and as a response to injury, are most unusual. Could the Uttwiler Spatlauber be the fruit of eternal life? What if the stem cells in these apples could enhance the longevity of human beings and animals? Could they retard the sad reality of aging or even prolong life? At Mibelle, a Swiss chemical lab, scientific tests demonstrated that the apple's cells actually protected human cells.

Like most fairy tales, this one might have a happy ending. A Scandinavian entrepreneur developed a skin cream incorporating the replicated cells of this almost extinct apple. Popularly known as Swiss Apple or Super Apple, it allegedly has an incredible ability to rejuvenate skin and capture an appearance of lost youth. Offered for sale at the price of $355.00 for a small jar, Michelle Obama, Helen Mirren, and Jennifer Lopez are reputedly among this cream's fans. Mrs. Obama has even written a complimentary letter, claims Francesco Clark, the botanist who formulated the cream. Apple based products intended to restore lost hair and darken grey hair are even being developed.

In 2008, the Swiss government paid tribute to the miraculous Uttwiler Spatlauber apple tree by putting it on a postage stamp. Today the grove has expanded to include at least seven trees. Perhaps in the future, there will even be enough of the magical apples available to eat. If the cream produced just by replicating the cells is so incredible, imagine what eating a whole Uttwiler Spatlauber apple in a Waldorf salad might do.

– ESTHER ELAYNE

Genius Loci

Spirit of place

EVERY locality has a unique character or atmosphere, its Genius Loci. That of coastal Rhode Island, for example, could be the intangible accumulation of salty sea air, cool sea breezes, and the dull hiss of waves crashing against the rocky shoreline. The ancients often concerned themselves with the Genius Loci. Saint Augustine wrote a great deal about the subject, particularly pertaining to gardens. He declared that the gardener should seek to honor the natural landscape, remaining true to the aspect suggested by rocks, trees, rivers or hills. In modern times the concept of Genius Loci has even been linked with the practice of *feng shui*, the most effective arrangement of objects for maximum energy flow.

The ancient Romans, from whom we receive the Latin phrase, also understood the Genius Loci literally. The "genius" refers to the attending protective spirit or godling of individual things. "Genius" differs from *anima*, or soul, in that *anima* is present in all things, whereas *genii* are individual spirits. *Genius Domus* was the spirit of the household; *Genius Familiae* of the family; Genius Loci, of particular natural places.

Cultures around the world have always understood that certain hills, caves and tunnels had their own protective spirits.

In Homer's *Iliad*, the hero Achilles fights the Genius of the River Xanthus. Consumed with blood lust, Achilles thoughtlessly casts his Trojan victims into the Xanthus. When the river's channels become choked with corpses and its rapids stained with blood, the Genius Loci rises up and asks Achilles to conduct his slaughter away from its banks. Achilles agrees, only to engage in battle directly with the river god. If not for the intercession of Poseidon and Athena, gods of much higher rank than the protector of Xanthus, Achilles would have been drowned for disrespecting the home of a Genius Loci.

The Celtic people also glimpsed protective fairy folk in specific locations. The *Sidhe*, or good folk, a race understood to be more than human but less than godly, live underground in hollowed-out hills or mounds. Other locations in Ireland may yield a Genius Loci. Any large leaning stone is said to house a *Grogoch*, a humanoid fairy covered in coarse red fur. *Clurichauns*, cousins of the Leprechaun, live in wine cellars. If offerings of wine are made to the *Clurichauns*, they will make sure the rest of your stock remains safe. However, anger a *Clurichaun* and count on sour wine for the rest of your life.

If your wine cellar is in Italy, the offering of wine should be made to the *Monacielli*, or little monks. Like the *Clurichauns*, these spirits when treated well will protect wine from harm. Italy in fact has a wealth of protective place spirits known in Italian as *Fata*. Walking the Italian countryside,

expect to encounter *Monachetto* in tunnels, *Orcuili* in caves, *Gianes* in woods, *Fauni* in fields, and *Aguane* in the mountains and rivers.

Wherever you travel, you will encounter a Genius Loci. It may be known as a *Sidhe* in Ireland, *Fata* in Italy or *Jinni* in the Arabic world. Every field or stream you pass may be home to a spirit, gnome or fairy keeping watch. These spirits, though sometimes mischievous and troublesome to unwitting people, serve the important role of protector. If not for these inhabiting spirits, every natural place would come under threat of exploitation and depletion. Now more than ever the guidance of these spirits is needed. A Genius Loci preserves the special characteristics and atmosphere of a place, keeping the world beautiful and interesting for the mortals who may otherwise destroy it.

– SHANNON MARKS

CENIVS HVIVSLOCI MONTIS

Death in the Roman World

The family bids farewell

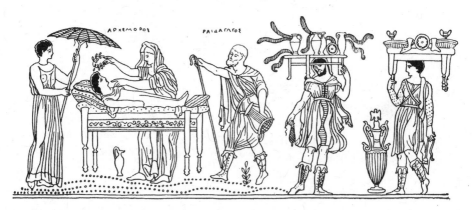

IN THE ancient Roman world, one's public reputation and the reputation of one's family was of primary importance. Citizens defined their self-worth and self-image by public opinion, as reflected by the community. The culture was strongly centered on the family, almost in a tribal sense. Religious practices were primarily held in the home, with a family altar dedicated to spirits that watched over the home and family: the Lares, depicted as a pair of youths who personified the genetic family line, the Penates, originally a pair of deities guarding the storeroom and provisions, and the Manes, spirits of the ancestors. Romans believed that these entities continued to have influence and honoring them was essential.

The families commemorated their dead with the best possible public face that could be afforded. With the exception of very young children and the destitute – quietly buried at night to avoid attention – funerary customs proclaimed the virtues of the deceased and the rectitude of the relatives.

A gold coin for the ferry

The ideal death occurred at home, surrounded by family. At the point of death, the person was placed on the ground and the last breath was caught with a kiss by a relative. The oldest son called the dead person's name three times. Then the deceased was washed, anointed with perfumed oils and dressed in his best clothing, including any earned emblems of rank or distinction. A gold coin was placed in the mouth to pay the ferryman Charon to convey the soul across the River Styx to the underworld. Souls who arrived at the riverbank without fare were doomed to wander the shore for a hundred years before being allowed to cross. No self-respecting family would want any of its relatives so disgraced. The deceased was laid out with his feet facing the door and the mourning began. The length

of time allowed for viewing varied with the importance of the deceased and the historic period (and, one might imagine, the weather). A modest citizen might be conveyed to the cemetery almost immediately, while others are recorded as being laid out for eight days.

Rites of passage

When the time came for the procession to the cemetery or tomb, the deceased was conveyed out the door feet first. The funeral procession was as lavish as the family could afford. For affluent families and illustrious individuals, the procession was announced by heralds and accompanied by musicians, dancers and professional mourning women. Next came the newly freed slaves of the deceased, the *liberti*.

Ahead of the corpse, relatives wore masks or carried busts representing the family's ancestors. If the deceased had been a person of prominence, the procession stopped at the Forum for an oration. One or more relatives, friends, associates or professional speakers delivered elegies proclaiming the decedent's virtues and accomplishments.

The funeral procession then continued to the place of burial, where the actual funeral took place. Although details of funeral services varied with the period, graveside rites always included three elements: the sanctification of the site, the casting of earth upon the remains, and the subsequent purification of persons and the home tainted by death. The casting of earth

was essential because Romans believed that the corpse must be buried before the spirit could be at peace. When cremation replaced interment, one bone, usually from a finger, was reserved for burial to satisfy this requisite.

Rituals performed at the grave included offerings of food and drink made for the dead and a luncheon for attendants. In cases of cremation, the ashes were extinguished with wine and then collected by a family member in a cloth to be dried.

Burial or cremation

Romans practiced both, with one or the other preferred at different times. In the last century of the Republic, cremation was favored, after Sulla (d.78 BCE) commanded that his remains be cremated. He wanted to assure prevention of bodily desecration as he had desecrated the body of his rival, Marius. Cremation remained in favor into the first century CE. By the fourth century CE, inhumation once again was preferred.

Romans cremated their dead on a pyre with possessions. The ashes could be buried in the cremation pit or removed to an urn and placed in a tomb.

Following the funeral, attendants and the home were sprinkled three times with water from an olive or laurel branch. A pig, associated with the

Underworld, was sacrificed, and the home was further purified with offerings to the Lares.

"Nine days of sorrow" began the day of cremation or burial. Citizens in mourning wore drab clothing, did not bathe, and neither cut nor combed their hair. Nine days after the remains were laid to rest, the family ended the funeral rites with the "sacrifice of the ninth day," another feast, and bid the deceased farewell, "vale."

Sites from parks to pits

Roman law required tombs and cemeteries to be located outside city limits. Wealthy families and prominent citizens built grand tombs lining the roads leading into cities, to provide the dead with some part in the hustle and bustle of life. Cemeteries, "cities of the dead," accommodated middle and elite classes. Some family burial grounds spread over several acres. These featured private parks with mausoleums, flower gardens, trees, fountains, pools, shelters, statues and strategically placed benches. The back sections of these memorial estates were often planted with food gardens, olive trees and vineyards to provide for memorial feasts and family picnics.

Families visited their cemeteries often, making the visit a relaxing day in the country with a picnic and leisurely

activities. In this way, they continued to include their deceased relatives in the activities of the living family.

Potter's field was considered the worst of all ends. During the Republic era (509 to 31 BCE), destitute dead were thrown outside the city in open pits serving as refuse dumps. To avoid the horror of a pauper's burial and secure a decent final resting place, Romans of modest means banded together and formed *collegia funeraticia*. These neighborhood funeral societies erected and maintained burial structures called *columbaria* (dovecotes), rather like condos for family remains. Members could purchase one or more niches for crematory urns. At small cost, nearly anyone could manage a decent, though modest, burial place.

Epitaphs and honors, violets and roses

Perhaps the most popular gravestone inscription for all classes was *dis manibus sacrem* (D.M.S.), "Sacred to the Ghost-gods" or "Gone Among the Spirits," referring to the Manes, spirits of the dead. *Hic situs est* or "he lies here" was another favorite. More elaborate epitaphs listed the virtues and accomplishments of the deceased.

Romans considered it tasteless to depict death too literally on tombstones. A horse's head was often seen as a motif that made oblique reference to the final journey. Tombs often illustrated images depicting the livelihood of the deceased, such as ships or grapes or bread. Tombs could be embellished with symbols representing virtues or talents, as well as classical ornamentation.

Families honored the memory of their dead with ongoing attention for several generations. Paternalia, a festival to honor the *divi parentes*, the deified ancestors, took place February 13th to 21st; the final day being Feralia. Paternalia was opened by the Vestal Virgins. Family members carried busts of their deceased relatives in a memorial parade through the streets. Offerings of wreaths, grain, salt, bread soaked in wine, and violets were placed at tombs to appease the dead. No marriages took place on Feralia, magistrates put off their insignia, and the gods were not worshipped that day.

At the end of March, on the Burial Day of the Dead, families honored the deceased again. Lemuria, yet another observance, took place on May 9th, 11th and 13th. Unlike the other annual festivals honoring ancestors, Lemuria was concerned with spiritual cleansing of the home. Family members performed ritual activities to appease and purge troubled spirits from the dwelling. The head of the household, walking barefoot through the house, spit out nine black beans, declaring with each, "These I send; with these beans I redeem me and mine." Family members clashed bronze pots and pans while responding each time, "Ghosts of our fathers and ancestors, be gone!" Because of its association with Lemuria, the month was considered an unlucky time to launch any new endeavor, including marriage. Things took a happier turn at the end of May, marking the end of the tainted month. In a final celebration known as the Vilolaria or Rosaria, violets and roses were distributed among relatives, and graves and urns were adorned with these flowers.

– Rhiannon McBride

White Alligators

The legend of living swamp ghosts

A SOUTHERN LEGEND tells us that people who can stare into the bright blue eyes of a rare kind of alligator will be blessed with incredible good luck. The evidence for this legend is strong enough so that for generations many have ventured into dangerous territory, risking life and limb to seek out these creatures.

About once in a century they do actually appear. This is just often enough to remain a part of living memory before it dissolves into myth and folklore. In 1987, deep in the bayous of Louisiana, a miracle occurred. A Cajun fisherman discovered a nest of eighteen newborns, only one of which was female. Today twelve are still alive. Four are housed in a comfortable, secure compound at Gatorland near Orlando, Florida. (The other eight are at the Audubon Zoo in New Orleans.)

The four Floridians have Cajun names, with English translations listed below on celebrity-style nameplates posted outside the private doors. Blan Bouya (White Fog), Jeyan Kwok (Giant Fang), Feros Zanbi (Fierce Ghost) and the last and largest of all, The Nameless One. They are pure white alligators. Because of a rare genetic trait called leucism, they are white without being albinos. Albino gators are quite common and they have pink eyes. But albinos tend to be fragile with deformed jaws and spines, and don't survive long.

The leucistic gators are completely unlike their weakling cousins. The true white alligators are exceptionally strong. Large and long lived, with striking electric-blue eyes, they are dangerous and bad tempered, even by alligator standards. They don't dwell in harmony with either each other or the commoners, those familiar brownish alligators. Visitors to the Orlando tourist corridor who have the opportunity to seek the vintage attractions of Old Time Florida can make a spiritual pilgrimage to see the white leucistic alligators and even exchange a lucky stare.

Where did the mysterious white alligators come from? Why are they so very rare? The wise ones of the bayou offer an interesting explanation. Long ago, when the world was younger, all the alligators were white. Arrogant and warlike, they felt invincible. Wily Rabbit was fed up with the situation and decided to play a trick.

Rabbit saw a swamp fire burning. He called out to the King of the White Gators and said, "There's the devil over there, I bet you're afraid of him."

Gator turned his cold blue eyes on the rabbit, telling Rabbit how stupid and ridiculous he was. "Of course I'm not afraid, the devil can't hurt me."

"You'd be afraid to go and see," answered Rabbit.

"Would not."

"Would too."

With that Gator walked straight into the flames, relentlessly ignoring the smoke and heat. He caught on fire, and yelped and screamed as he turned a toasty brown. Even his eyes became brown and murky. Ever since then, almost all alligators have been brown, humbled and fooled by wily Rabbit.

– MARINA BRYONY

𝔄 𝔇𝔞𝔰𝔥 𝔬𝔣 𝔖𝔞𝔩𝔱 ⊖

Humor is like salt on meat. A little makes all things palatable.

–Native American Proverb

SALT has been vital to every known civilization on the planet. Used as a preservative since antiquity, the magnitude of its importance is astonishing. The curative and mystical powers of salt are legendary the world over.

Salt is a relic from the ancient oceans, the source of all life. Only a little salt is required to keep a living organism alive, yet that dash is absolutely essential to survival itself. Salt transmits an electrical charge that maintains the fluid balance in cells, the homeostasis. The chemical composition of the human body (75% water, and ideally less than 1% salt) is very similar to ocean water. Perhaps this is why time spent along the sea coast is associated with healing and rejuvenation.

Salt is emblematic of enlightenment, purification and intervention. Newborn babies were once rubbed with salt, partly as a medicinal treatment but also to ward off the evil eye. Salt has been a key ingredient in medicines throughout the ages. The wisest witches often carry a small envelope of salt as an easy and effective talisman against danger and negativity.

Worth one's salt

By 2700 BCE, forty different kinds of salt were recorded in various Chinese writings. Slaves were exchanged for salt in ancient Greece, while in Slavic countries a bride and groom were traditionally given salt to ensure health and happiness. Roman soldiers were paid partly in salt, hence the origin of the word "salary" which derives from a root word meaning "salt." The Ethiopians created coins of salt for use as currency. Being "worth one's salt" is another reference linking salt to money.

The French Revolution was fueled by a tax on salt and many of Napoleon's soldiers perished from a lack of salt while retreating from Russia. In the United States, the Erie Canal was constructed mainly to ship salt.

Sacred salt

Holy offerings and sacred water have long been blessed with salt. The ancient Egyptians, Brahmans, and Greeks included salt in rituals of sacrifice, while the Hittites and Semites threw it into sacred fires, creating a crackling sound that seems to have been part of its symbolic significance. The Aztecs worshiped the salt goddess Huixtocihuatl.

"Salted" is a Biblical reference signifying the longing for truth. Free will has often been called "the salt of devotion." In alchemy, salt relates to the basic principle of earth and solidity. Hermetic philosophy further teaches that it is also the equilibrium of mercury and sulfur.

Pink salt, dark salt

Lamps fashioned from a pink salt mined in the Himalayas are popular today. Warmed and illuminated with small bulbs, they are thought to create a cleansing and peaceful atmosphere. The indigenous people of the area use the salt to ward off demons.

Salt also has its dark side. Fresh water that became a salt marsh was thought to be the result of a curse, and conquering generals such as Scipio Africanus and Attila the Hun were known to salt the fields of their enemies, creating barren fields, both symbolically and literally.

Salt dreams

Dreams involving salt may represent the spiritual essence of life. A dream may show tears releasing sorrow, as tears always taste of salt. A dream might also indicate that someone or something is "rubbing salt in a wound." Other popular interpretations of the appearance of salt within a dream include a warning against food poisoning and surprises in romance.

Common salt (NaCl or sodium chloride) crystallizes in a cubic pattern and lowers the freezing temperature of water. It is used during the winter to prevent vehicles and pedestrians from slipping on icy roads and sidewalks. Laundry detergent, refrigeration fluid, many processed foods, concrete and numerous other items familiar in daily life all require salt.

Salt confers wisdom and tact

The trend toward adding large amounts of salt to food began during the time of Queen Elizabeth I. This is because on Wednesdays and Fridays, Her Majesty insisted that her subjects eat fish. Today health experts warn of the risks of an over salted diet. Legal mandates are even being considered to regulate the amount of salt in prepared foods.

Since salt enhances the flavor of food, this brings to mind another instance of taste-related symbolism. "Tasteless" is a synonym for foolish, but also means without salt. The joke is that salt confers both wisdom and tact. St. Paul therefore encouraged the faithful to "season their words with salt," hinting that salt might be the ultimate weapon in winning a battle of wits.

– ELAINE NEUMEIER

Moon Cycles

A New Moon rises with the Sun,
Her waxing half at midday shows,
The Full Moon climbs at sunset hour,
And waning half the midnight knows.

NEW	2012	FULL	NEW	2013	FULL
January 23		January 9	January 11		January 26
February 21		February 7	February 10		February 25
March 22		March 8	March 11		March 27
April 21		April 6	April 10		April 25
May 20		May 5	May 9		May 25
June 19		June 4	June 8		June 23
July 19		July 3	July 8		July 22
August 17		Aug. 1, 31 (Blue Moon)	August 6		August 20
September 15		September 29	September 5		September 19
October 15		October 29	October 4		October 18
November 13		November 28	November 3		November 17
December 13		December 28	December 2		December 17

Life takes on added dimension when you
match your activities to the waxing and waning of the Moon.
Observe the sequence of her phases to learn
the wisdom of constant change within complete certainty.

presage

by Dikki-Jo Mullen

ARIES 2011 — PISCES 2012

THE BIRTH chart is a cosmic map showing the limits and strengths of an individual's nature. Astrology's message is to "make the most of yourself, for that is all there is of you."

Begin Presage by reading your familiar Sun sign, which shows how you express your identity. Then consult the pages devoted to your Moon sign for insight on your emotional needs and those on your rising sign for a deeper awareness of how others see you. The retrogrades and eclipses section offers understanding of cycles with a more universal impact.

The year ahead brings five eclipses. Three are clustered together on June 1, June 15, and July 1. Expect many surprising events during the spring and summer. On July 30 a rare Black Moon (the second new Moon in a single month) ushers in a mystical mood. Two more eclipses on November 25 and December 10 dramatically affect the holiday season.

Neptune begins the year in its ruling sign of Pisces, then retrogrades back over the Aquarius cusp on August 4. Finally on February 3, 2012 Neptune enters Pisces for a 14-year passage, the first such transit since 1847. This can impact water supply, rainfall, and our appreciation of aquatic creatures.

From November 11, 2011 through the end of winter a grand trine in Earth signs involving Mars in Virgo, Jupiter in Taurus, and Pluto in Capricorn is present. We will all learn to adjust to the new global economic situation. All year long serious Saturn moves slowly through Libra, its sign of exaltation, promoting fairness, improved manners, and more consideration for others.

ASTROLOGICAL KEYS

Signs of the Zodiac
Channels of Expression

ARIES: fiery, pioneering, competitive
TAURUS: earthy, stable, practical
GEMINI: dual, lively, versatile
CANCER: protective, traditional
LEO: dramatic, flamboyant, warm
VIRGO: conscientious, analytical
LIBRA: refined, fair, sociable
SCORPIO: intense, secretive, ambitious
SAGITTARIUS: friendly, expansive
CAPRICORN: cautious, materialistic
AQUARIUS: inquisitive, unpredictable
PISCES: responsive, dependent, fanciful

Elements

FIRE: Aries, Leo, Sagittarius
EARTH: Taurus, Virgo, Capricorn
AIR: Gemini, Libra, Aquarius
WATER: Cancer, Scorpio, Pisces

Qualities

CARDINAL	FIXED	MUTABLE
Aries	Taurus	Gemini
Cancer	Leo	Virgo
Libra	Scorpio	Sagittarius
Capricorn	Aquarius	Pisces

CARDINAL signs mark the beginning of each new season — active.
FIXED signs represent the season at its height — steadfast.
MUTABLE signs herald a change of season — variable.

Celestial Bodies
Generating Energy of the Cosmos

Sun: birth sign, ego, identity
Moon: emotions, memories, personality
Mercury: communication, intellect, skills
Venus: love, pleasures, the fine arts
Mars: energy, challenges, sports
Jupiter: expansion, religion, happiness
Saturn: responsibility, maturity, realities
Uranus: originality, science, progress
Neptune: dreams, illusions, inspiration
Pluto: rebirth, renewal, resources

Glossary of Aspects

Conjunction: two planets within the same sign or less than 10 degrees apart, favorable or unfavorable according to the nature of the planets.

Sextile: a pleasant, harmonious aspect occurring when two planets are two signs or 60 degrees apart.

Square: a major negative effect resulting when planets are three signs from one another or 90 degrees apart.

Trine: planets four signs or 120 degrees apart, forming a positive and favorable influence.

Quincunx: a mildly negative aspect produced when planets are five signs or 150 degrees apart.

Opposition: a six sign or 180 degrees separation of planets generating positive or negative forces depending on the planets involved.

The Houses — *Twelve Areas of Life*

1st house: appearance, image, identity
2nd house: money, possessions, tools
3rd house: communications, siblings
4th house: family, domesticity, security
5th house: romance, creativity, children
6th house: daily routine, service, health

7th house: marriage, partnerships, union
8th house: passion, death, rebirth, soul
9th house: travel, philosophy, education
10th house: fame, achievement, mastery
11th house: goals, friends, high hopes
12th house: sacrifice, solitude, privacy

Eclipses

Natal horoscopes as well as charts of important world events are profoundly affected by eclipses. Surprises, a fresh start, and a change in the balance of power are part of the celestial drama which unfolds with this phenomenon. Be flexible and observant during an eclipse. Avoid haste and risks. Those who celebrate a birthday within three days of an eclipse can anticipate a very interesting year. There are five eclipses during the year ahead.

June 1, 2011   New Moon Solar in Gemini, south node – partial
June 15, 2011   Full Moon Lunar in Sagittarius, north node – total
July 1, 2011   New Moon Solar in Cancer, south node – partial
November 25, 2011   New Moon Solar in Sagittarius, north node – partial
December 10, 2011   Full Moon Lunar in Gemini, south node – total

Retrograde Planetary Motion

Occasionally the planets appear to be moving backward in their orbits. Although this is an illusion created by the relative motion of the Earth, the impact is felt. Retrograde motion is no less significant than direct motion. Matters which are ruled by the retrograde planet are impacted most.

Mercury Retrograde Cycle

Retrograde Mercury creates a stir with technology, travel schedules, missed appointments, and communication of all kinds. It also brings renewed contact from those who have been out of touch. Complete old projects, revise and review, and tread familiar paths. Enjoy a reunion or a past life regression. Residential moves or job changes undertaken while Mercury is retrograde may lack stability. Be especially cautious in making promises or signing binding contracts. The Mercury-ruled signs of Gemini and Virgo are especially affected, while individuals born with Mercury retrograde will thrive.

March 31–April 24, 2011 in Aries

August 3–27, 2011 in Virgo and Leo

November 25–December 14, 2011
in Sagittarius

March 13, 2012 –
through the winter's end in Aries

Mars Retrograde Cycle

Just before Candlemas through the end of winter Mars is retrograde in Virgo. Expect tension in repeating cycles regarding health and daily employment. Employ strategy in peacefully resolving conflict. The aggressor is always the loser when Mars is retrograde; injurious intentions will rebound upon the perpetrator. The military, sports, surgery, fire, energy, hunting, manufacturing, and construction are all ruled by Mars and can be topics of concern. Because they are ruled by Mars, Aries and Scorpio people will especially sense this change of energy levels.

January 24, 2012 –
through the winter's end in Virgo

ARIES
The year ahead for those
born under the sign of the Ram
March 20–April 19

Being last is never an option for Aries. This Mars-ruled sign radiates impetuous charm and youthful enthusiasm. Aries blossoms when involved in new ventures. But taking initiative can mean that a bit of impatience must be overcome before success is achieved. The tiger's eye agate is an earth stone that will aid in making this happen. The tiger's eye has been carried by warriors since early Roman times to assure courage and victory.

It's a spring season of travel and ideas. Because of a retrograde cycle Mercury remains in your sign from the vernal equinox through May 15. Make plans to complete or continue study programs. From April 3 until mid-May it's a time of great motivation and promise, for Mars races alongside Mercury and Jupiter; Venus joins in on April 21. Express creative talents and pursue your wildest dreams as this exceptional stellium in your sign peaks on May Eve.

May finds you seeking stability. A strong, earthy 2nd house influence accents earning power and security issues. During June, Saturn, which is in opposition to you all year, changes direction in your 7th house of relationships. Commitments to others, the plans and needs of partners, will enter a new phase by Midsummer's Day. The solar eclipse on July 1 is angular, in your 4th house. It immediately brings residence and family issues to the fore. Remodeling or moving is possible. The structure of family life is in flux. Gracefully accept the fact that family ties change as time passes.

By Lammastide, Venus is in Leo, your sister fire sign, where it remains until August 21, highlighting your love and pleasure sector. Plan a vacation, perhaps including a romantic rendezvous. August 28 – September 9 Mercury trines your Sun, favoring communication with loved ones and creative writing projects. Through Mabon favorable earth sign influences support your 6th house. Natural remedies can improve health; daily employment opportunities are more plentiful. Late September is brightened by the unconditional love offered by animal friends. On October 11 the Full Moon in your sign activates several cardinal sign planets, including Saturn and Uranus. Associates may enter and leave your life suddenly in the weeks before Samhain. Revel in momentary joys and relish the present. Impermanence is the keynote now. A dream near Halloween provides insight into a past life.

On November 9 Neptune turns direct in your 11th house bringing new clarity to personal goals. A friend suggests charitable projects or deeper community involvement. The eclipse pattern of late November and December accents a new state of mind and new interests. At Yule the Sun enters Capricorn and conjoins Pluto. Both march toward a square aspect with Uranus in Aries. Endings and beginnings must be balanced. Be alert to new trends in your professional sector. As 2012 begins Venus joins Neptune to make a friendly sextile aspect lasting through January 14. Networking leads to opportunity. Friends can truly be a blessing during the weeks preceding Candlemas. Your 12th house is strong during the last half of the month. Take time to meditate; a quiet mind knows the right answer.

From February 9 – March 5 Venus brings genuine sparkle. It moves rapidly through your sign, in conjunction with Uranus. A new friend offers valuable ideas. Social and financial prospects are better. From March 3 through winter's end Mercury enters Aries and hovers in a wide cardinal T-square before turning retrograde on March 13. Look to precedent and experience for wise insight. A second chance is offered. A reunion may be planned.

HEALTH

Near your birthday Mars and Jupiter conjoin your natal Sun. This is great for overcoming negative health habits. Try developing expertise in a sport, with the goal of it positively affecting your health. By November 12 Mars, your ruler, enters Virgo, the sign on your 6th house of health. Mars remains through the end of winter, turning retrograde on January 24. Take preventative measures to protect your health during this time. Good or bad, your ongoing health history repeats in early 2012.

LOVE

Uranus has crossed the Aries cusp and entered your sign for a seven-year stay. It is in a wide orb of opposition to Saturn in Libra, the sign of relationships. One of the most interesting and unpredictable times you will ever know regarding love is about to commence. Friends and lovers can change roles; you can connect with gifted and eccentric new people. If an existing relationship survives it will most likely be approached in a new way. Venus aspects light the way for this all to result in happiness during late April to mid-May, the first three weeks of August, and from early February – March 5.

SPIRITUALITY

June 15 and November 25 bring eclipses in your 9th house of spirituality. Set aside these dates for spiritual activities. A new guru or teacher can offer intriguing new perspectives before the year ends. Studying another language or visiting a sacred site may play a role in your spiritual awakening. Investigate Native American lore, especially sacred fire ceremonies and observations honoring sunrises and sunsets.

FINANCE

Jovial and generous Jupiter greets you on your birthday with a conjunction to your Sun. Jupiter remains in Aries until June 4 before entering your 2nd house of cash flow for the rest of the year. Don't be overly optimistic or gamble. If you don't overextend you should have a very good year financially. It's a time to recognize and build upon promising new opportunities which present themselves. Financial decisions made now can favorably affect you for many years to come.

TAURUS
The year ahead for those
born under the sign of the Bull
April 20 – May 20

Stability is the very essence of life for Taurus. Changes forced before you're ready to accept them is akin to waving a red cloth in the face of the Bull. A deep-rooted need for security and appreciation for nature's beauty characterize this sign. Although officially ruled by comfort-loving Venus, many astrologers feel Earth itself could be a co-ruler of Taurus. The moss agate is your earth stone. Fortunate for gardeners to wear or carry, the moss agate is a beautiful, variegated stone in rich shades of green.

Friends offer challenges and stimulating ideas during spring's earliest days. A Mars sextile involving your sector of associates and goals sets the pace through All Fool's Day. The remainder of April you'll feel the urge to keep a low profile. Mercury joins Jupiter and Uranus in your 12th house of secrets. There is much you would prefer not to reveal. Dreams near the Full Moon of April 17 could offer insight into maintaining your well-being by May Eve. By May 16 Venus and Mercury enter Taurus and move toward a trine with Pluto. Travel, new career and study opportunities, and solutions to difficult financial situations are in the wind. Your life moves forward.

On June 4 Jupiter enters your sign and remains through the rest of the year. Prepare for growth. From the summer solstice through Lammas Mars highlights your 2nd house of finances and possessions. You'll feel motivated to acquire long-desired possessions while pouring extra effort into enhancing your financial security. Starting on Independence Day, Mercury races through your home and family sector and remains there the rest of July. Relatives offer ideas about interior decorating, family travel, and household dynamics.

During August and September cardinal sign transits strongly aspect Saturn in your 6th house. Animal companions may require extra understanding. Before adopting a new pet, ask yourself whether it will be suitable. This cycle also brings an urge for greater organization and cleanliness amid disorder. Patiently organize one area at a time. From late September through mid-October the Sun, Venus, and Mercury join Saturn in your wellness sector. It's an ideal time to try sound and color healing or other alternative therapies. Relax and be aware of how stress affects you.

From October 10 through All Hallows an interesting Venus opposition brings gifted, attractive people into your life. Be receptive to invitations. All Soul's Day ushers in a strong emphasis on your 8th house, the sector of spirituality and the afterlife. Study reincarnation; following a hunch can reveal a past life experience. The Taurus Full Moon on November 10 makes you pleasantly aware of how much you are accomplishing. Following this lunation Mars begins an upbeat passage through Virgo, your sister Earth sign, and the ruler of your love and pleasure sector. This lasts through the end of the winter. Expect progress in sports or in pursuing a cherished hobby. The attention you put into an intimate relationship results in an important choice regarding love. A child can need extra attention – the efforts you make now can favorably impact a young person's whole future. Make time.

Yuletide finds Venus joining Neptune in your 10th house. Social contacts can impact your credibility. Elements of fate and fantasy affect your career. Expressing imaginative ideas assures success. During January a grand trine in Earth signs is activated by a rapidly moving Mercury. Your sector of travel, religion, and academic pursuits benefits from this exceptionally positive influence. If you've always wanted to write or enroll in classes, now is the time. Near Candlemas the emphasis shifts and you'll be drawn toward altruistic interests. Cupid brings a belated Valentine when Venus enters Taurus on March 5, where it remains through early spring. Seek favors and express heartfelt connections as the year ends.

HEALTH

Solemn Saturn moves slowly through your health sector the year long. Patience is essential in reaching health goals. Be aware of habits and heredity in health matters. Since the sign of Libra is involved, maintaining balance between personal and professional pursuits is a must, as is maintaining a healthy weight. The autumn brings turning points in health, good or bad.

The consequences of how you've treated your body will be felt.

LOVE

Venus dances through the Earth signs, favoring you with happiness from May 15 – June 9, August 22 – September 14, from Thanksgiving through Yuletide, and again from March 5 – winter's end of 2012. Cultivate love prospects then. Select the perfect gift for one whom you would woo beneath the light of the Full Moon in Taurus on November 10. A crystal goblet, fine essential oils, or a bonsai tree would be sure to please.

SPIRITUALITY

Jupiter transits your sign starting on June 4. This can generate some deeply spiritual experiences, especially near the high holidays. Take time to plan observances of the sabbats with greater care. When Jupiter aspects Pluto during June and July 2011 and again in March 2012, deeper spiritual experiences can occur. Earth stones, crystals, and connections with the Earth elementals can be part of this. Watch for gnomes.

FINANCE

The eclipse pattern this year profoundly impacts both your 2nd and 8th houses. Earnings, taxes, insurance coverage, investments, cash flow, and inherited resources are involved. There can be surprise gains and losses; be aware of new financial trends. Your income might come from a different source. June – July and November – December will bring the specifics to light. A strong Earth sign influence promises a favorable outcome following some highs and lows.

GEMINI
The year ahead for those
born under the sign of the Twins
May 21–June 20

Skilled and consistent communicators, Geminis are surrounded by words and ideas. The bright and bubbly Twin is complex and can appear happy even if feeling troubled or depressed inwardly. An affinity with movement and action creates a lifelong aura of youthfulness. The citrine, found in lovely shades of yellow and orange, is your earth stone. Citrine relates to communication and mental clarity.

Spring begins with a gentle Venus–Neptune conjunction in a trine aspect to your Sun. An eloquent message or invitation from a loved one arrives. Travel could be involved. It's a wonderful time to pen a poem or short story. Mercury, your ruler, goes retrograde by All Fool's Day, impacting your 11th house of friendships, goals, and group affiliations through April 24. Avoid making binding commitments right now, especially to serve on the boards of clubs or organizations. The Full Moon of April 11 can bring news from a lost love. Some confusion follows. Gather information before responding. As Beltane nears, longtime relationships and familiar situations may suddenly bore you. New associates and different goals become a bigger part

of your life now. It's essential for you to simplify, focus, and decide what is really important. During May you can find deep satisfaction in volunteer work. Helping those less fortunate can dispel personal frustration. Meditation and dream messages help you attune to subconscious needs.

As your birthday approaches, your gift of gab will be in top form, as Mercury and Venus join the Sun in your 1st house during early June. Your sparkling personality opens new doors. Travel plans and a busy schedule fill the weeks leading to Midsummer's Day. The eclipses on June 1, June 15, and July 1 promise profound changes impacting partnerships, personal needs, and your values. From late June to the first few days of August, Mars moves rapidly through your sign. The cosmic warrior aspects first Saturn then Neptune, creating a favorable grand trine in air signs. A sense of purpose guides you toward worthwhile goals this summer. Exercise provides a perfect release near Lammastide. The Mercury retrograde August 3 – 27 affects your 3rd and 4th houses. A vehicle might need service or replacement; be aware of events in your neighborhood which could affect you. Stay on top of home repairs.

Early September brings a more benign influence in your home and family sector. Situations regarding relatives grow more relaxed. The last half of September features a gathering of planets including Saturn, Venus, the Sun, and Mercury in your love and pleasure sector. A new relationship or interesting avocation adds sparkle to the start of autumn. Share your ideas; the support of someone you admire can propel you forward through mid-October. As All Hallows nears, a new interest in health arises. Get plenty of fresh water, juices, and healing teas. Add healthy humidity to a dry room by simmering water with a handful of peppermint or other fragrant herbs.

During November your sector of justice and balance is affected by Sagittarius transits and an eclipse. Get both sides of every story; weigh all issues with care and attention to detail. The Thanksgiving weekend promises surprise announcements from others. December brings a total eclipse of the Full Moon in your sign. A major move of job or residence may be brewing. January 1 – 14 finds Venus transiting your 9th house. A friendship with a foreign-born or very intellectual friend can lead to romance. By Candlemas supportive Sun and Mercury influences give you greater vitality and clarity of thought. Enjoy this time of progress and accomplishment.

From Valentine's Day through the end of the winter you'll feel Neptune's shift as it moves over your midheaven into the 10th house where it will remain for many years. A time of redefining your status and career is due. The Pisces New Moon on February 21 favors divination and magical workings regarding vocational goals. A hunch or creative idea can help. Once Mercury turns retrograde on March 13, relax and reflect on days past.

HEALTH
Solar eclipses in June and December promise some changes in vitality this year. Listen to and heed your body's needs. Avoid negative people who are psychic vampires. You must conserve your energy and not allow it to be drained. Mars makes a long passage through your 4th house from November 11 through the end of winter. Use this time to fortify your domestic environment, making it safe and wholesome.

LOVE
Stability and loyalty will be important in love, as sober Saturn is in your 5th house all year long. At the same time, June and November bring eclipses in your 7th house of committed partnerships. There can be a turning point in relationships. Expect either a new cycle involving an existing tie or a change in your needs regarding love, leading to something new.

SPIRITUALITY
The runes have a traditional link to Woden, another face of Mercury. With a total eclipse in your sign in December, Yuletide will be intensely spiritual. Dedicate a set of runes to the Norns and delve into the Northern Mysteries. Gather fresh mistletoe to hang high in your dwelling. Burn bayberry candles at Yule.

FINANCE
Jupiter, planet of wealth, is dignified by its placement in your 12th house the year long. This is called the "guardian angel influence" in traditional astrology. You'll have access to favors and opportunities which will address your needs. The eclipse of July 1 falls in your financial sector; be receptive to new sources of income. Adapt to the changing economic situation and all will be well.

CANCER
The year ahead for those
born under the sign of the Crab
June 21–July 22

Sympathetic and caring, Cancer tends to look after others. Your home can be a cozy retreat filled with sentimental keepsakes. Enjoy your collectibles, but keep the temptation to hoard in check. An acute sensitivity is present, often bringing an imaginative expression of ideas and a gift of profound insight. There can be mood swings though. The moonstone is your earth stone. Moonstones enhance intuition, psychic dreams, and emotional balance.

A sense of urgency prevails as spring begins. A potent cardinal T-square involving Pluto, Jupiter, Uranus, the Sun, and Saturn affects you. Much can be accomplished, but you must focus and release stress in order to do your best. A new position of leadership can be offered unexpectedly. The first three weeks of April bring a favorable Venus influence. Travel, friendships with those from different cultures can build; it's a great time for creative writing and other artistic pursuits. At Beltane five planets cluster in your 10th house. You'll be highly visible, so be cognizant of image and reputation. During the last half of May supportive aspects from Mars and Mercury bring encouragement from others. Relieve stress with humor and close friends.

During June visualization and written affirmations can be very helpful. The eclipses on the 1st and 15th can affect physical and emotional health. Get several opinions about health-related decisions. A beloved animal companion offers solace. Mercury moves through your sign from mid-June to early July. This is wonderful for travel, making plans, and all kinds of study and communication. The July 1 eclipse promises turning points and shifts in the status quo. Watch for an opportunity to try something new. By Fourth of July, Venus is in your sign, where it remains until just before Lammas. Social and cultural events highlight the summer. Be receptive to a new romantic prospect near your birthday.

August finds your 2nd house strong. Financial issues come to the fore. Fashion a prosperity ritual using honey, cinnamon, gold, and a green candle just before the Full Moon of August 13. A spirit guide, maybe in the form of a departed loved one, can appear to offer financial counsel. Just after Lammastide, Mars enters your sign, where it remains until September 18. Control anger and impatience at all costs. At the same time, this trend does bring the precious gift of vitality. Plans can be laid for the long-term future; others will be amazed by how much you accomplish in a short time. Be a good sport if a situation becomes competitive.

At Mabon home decor and family dynamics are emphasized. Consider home improvements. Family members want to be closer; happy memories can be created during the weeks before All Hallows. October 10 – November 2 is a promising cycle for romance as Venus highlights your 5th house of love. The New Moon on October 26 brings this influence to the fore. November finds your 6th house highlighted by several planets as well as the eclipse on the 25th. Wellness factors and getting organized are the focus. It's an excellent time to plan a dumb supper or traditional séance. The veil to the other side is very thin and spiritual messages can come easily. Adopt a live-and-let-live attitude in December. The eclipse on the 10th combined with a series of mutable sign transits can make those near you restless and uncertain. Offer suggestions, but keep expectations in check. At Yule a ritual oriented toward loyalty and sincerity would be apropos.

The Full Moon in Cancer on January 9 brings an increasing awareness of your roots. The last half of February finds Mercury favorably placed in your travel sector. If a journey abroad is desired this is a good time to either make plans or to depart. An influential book appears which offers helpful new perspectives. Winter's final days find Saturn retrograde in the home and family sector. A chance for reprieve arrives regarding housing and family matters.

HEALTH

A tremendous emphasis on cardinal signs the year long promises a hectic cycle. Taking time for stress release is a must. Don't engage in any hazardous activities when preoccupied or angry. This is especially true near the time of the solar eclipse on July 1 and while Mars is in Cancer during August and September.

LOVE

With Pluto in the midst of a long transit through your 7th house of relationships, a great deal of transformation and intensity surrounds the whole topic of commitment. Don't be tempted by addictive love. July and October bring promising Venus aspects. Love can bloom then. This is true again from January 14 – February 8 when Venus moves into a favorable trine aspect.

SPIRITUALITY

Mystical Neptune is making a rare sign change this year. Retrograding back and forth over the Aquarius – Pisces cusp to finally begin a 14-year stay in Pisces on February 3, this ushers in a deeply spiritual cycle. The sixth sense is heightened; synchronicities and dreams are important factors. Travel and study can be a part of spiritual growth because the 9th house is activated.

FINANCE

Through early June an extravagant square from Jupiter suggests bargain hunting and avoiding risks. Don't splurge. Recycle and make do. Once the Cancer eclipse has passed on July 1 financial stresses can ease. Favorable earth and water sign transits in October promote resolving monetary issues and adding to savings. Be careful not to overspend on home improvements due to Saturn's placement in your 4th house all year. Keep receipts and check the references of those with whom you do business.

LEO
The year ahead for those
born under the sign of the Lion
July 23–August 22

Leos prowl the zodiac with pride and dignity, yet manage to be affectionate and playful at the same time. Ruled by the Sun and linked with the element fire, you emit a warm and demonstrative energy. Your leadership ability is combined with a generous streak of creativity. Amber is your earth stone. Cooling anger and impatience, amber facilitates balance between the head and heart. It also guards against heatstroke.

Spring's first days find Venus in your 7th house of partnerships. One whom you cherish celebrates a success. Graciously allow them to take center stage. By the New Moon in Aries on April 3 a grouping of planets affects your 9th house. Write a wish list of desires you would like to manifest. An exceptionally benevolent series of aspects takes effect during early to mid-April. Enjoy adventure, travel, educational pursuits, and cementing bonds with those of another generation. An old hurdle is overcome by May Eve. During May there is a focus on competitive career situations. Your motivation is high, but a square from Mercury is present. Diplomacy is essential in delicate negotiations; use care in making promises.

Jupiter changes signs during June, moving toward a square with your Sun which lasts through the end of the year. The gambler and rogue within you surfaces. By Midsummer's Eve you'll be at the center of attention – make sure this generates celebrity rather than notoriety. During most of July, Mercury races through your sign. Accept opportunities for public speaking or sharing your written thoughts. Your natural eloquence opens new doors. Devote the New Moon in Leo on July 30 and Lammastide rituals to Venus; she conjoins your Sun from then until August 21. Romance as well as financial situations will be exceptionally positive near your birthday.

Security and cash flow issues highlight early September. From just before Mabon through Samhain, Mars blazes through your sign. Much can be accomplished if you combine analytical ability and forethought with the actions you initiate at this time. From November 3 – January 8 Mercury makes a long passage through your 5th house. An old love can return near the time of the solar eclipse on November 25. Children are a source of both joy and concern during the darkest days of winter. This entire cycle brings invitations to travel and visit. January 1 – 7 is the best time to venture into unfamiliar territory.

Health and fitness factors surface during the last three weeks of January. Pluto is involved, so it's the perfect time to transform any negative habits. Try to schedule body work near the Full

Moon in your sign on February 7. By Valentine's Day, Venus joins Uranus in a sizzling fire sign combo. A dinner of fine foreign cuisine followed by mystical music or a foreign film can set the stage for a memorable time with one you would woo. The late winter finds Mars retrograde in your financial sector. Be patient if negotiating a pay raise. Employ humor and perspective if anger builds around a financial issue. Late February – early March has Mercury and the Sun opposing Mars. Financial planning, inheritances, taxes, investment income can be sources of concern. The Full Moon on March 8 can bring the specifics to light. Be wary of advice that contradicts your better judgment regarding money. The last two weeks of winter find Venus and Jupiter moving into a conjunction, bringing refinement and charm to your 10th house of fame and fortune. A fan helps brighten your status. Career circumstances are more comfortable. Hosting a party for coworkers sometime during March is a great option for making the best of this benevolent influence.

HEALTH

Pluto sits in your health sector all year in square to Uranus. Cardinal signs are involved, so focus on the present. This is the perfect time to take stock of exactly what is happening with wellness factors and to get started on needed lifestyle changes. Take special care to protect your health while traveling. A spiritual text could bring healing or offer health-related insights during July and in late winter.

LOVE

The eclipses on June 15 and November 25 both fall in your 5th house of love. Near those dates there can be surprises regarding the course of true love. A strong existing relationship can move to a new level of intimacy or a new love can suddenly replace a stale situation. A love ritual invoking dragon magic would be very effective. Seek a statue or drawing of a favorite dragon, then create a love altar featuring it. Bless a dragon's egg earth stone to offer as a token to true love.

SPIRITUALITY

All year long, Neptune hovers on the Aquarius-Pisces cusp, your 8th house, indicating a need for deeper meaning in spiritual work. In early February, Neptune finally enters Pisces, to remain for the next 14 years. This shows that late winter could bring a meaningful visitation from a loved one or entity from the spirit world. A personal near-death experience can occur, leaving a new sense of spiritual peace and insight in its wake.

FINANCE

A good Jupiter influence favors a risky gamble or expansion from the spring equinox through June 2. Friends mean well, but the mutable sign eclipses on June 1 and December 10 square a long Mars transit through your 2nd house of finances toward the end of the year. Don't be drawn into a financial scheme by a pal; it would be disappointing in the long run. Since the sign of Gemini is involved, affirmations could be very helpful.

VIRGO
The year ahead for those
born under the sign of the Virgin
August 23-September 22

You're a gifted and reliable trouble-shooter, sought after for your critical and analytical abilities. Tidiness and order are the passions of the Virgin. Ruled by clever Mercury, Virgo excels at communication, loves to travel, and is endlessly fascinated by health. The carnelian agate is Virgo's special talisman. It relates to all kinds of healing and has a traditional link to the spiritual traditions of India.

Spring begins with Mars, then Venus moving in opposition aspect to your Sun. Associates are very focused on you. This can be stimulating, but a little unsettling. Encourage good humored tolerance with those who seem too demanding. Since Mercury will be retrograde in your 8th house there may be a mystery to solve at the same time. By April 24 this trend runs its course. Several planets, including Jupiter, hover in your 8th house through May, showing income from investments. You'll have access to needed funds.

From May 11 until before the summer solstice, Mars trines your Sun. Physical activity will uplift and improve your mind. The triple eclipse pattern of June and July promises change in your schedule both at work and at home. When this culminates on July 1, completely new long-term goals can emerge. Be progressive; clinging to the past does not serve you well as summer commences. Just after Independence Day, Venus moves into a pleasant aspect involving your 11th house. Membership in a civic organization can be deeply satisfying. A new circle of friends is forming. Be receptive, accept invitations, and explore different events.

A short journey is favored at the end of July through Lammastide when Mercury will be in your sign. August 3 it goes retrograde, soon moving back into your 12th house where it remains through September 8. Appreciate peace and privacy; it's better to say less and listen more. The last three weeks of September again favor travel, perhaps as part of a birthday celebration. During October the Sun and other Libra transits join Saturn in your financial sector. It's a good time to accept extra employment and decrease overhead. Samhain emphasizes communication. A powerful ritual chant reinforces the sacred truths as this darkest quarter of the year begins.

In mid-November, Mars enters your sign for a long passage lasting through the end of winter. This gives you great energy and motivation, yet also brings a tendency to be a bit angry and argumentative. Maintain good humor and much can be accomplished. Mars aspects the mutable sign eclipses on November 25 and December 10, affecting the angles of your horoscope profoundly. A new residence or career path is possible. Family dynamics are shifting, as is the balance of power in your professional life. This can attract extra recognition, as the north node is in the 10th house of fame, supporting the December eclipse. At Yuletide, Jupiter is about to complete its retrograde and the Sun joins Pluto in Capricorn. The New Moon on December 24 brings an especially upbeat note to your romance and pleasure sector. The promise of new options brings hope and happiness into your life as 2012 begins.

January 9 – 27 a Mercury aspect favors problem solving and can bring an invitation to travel with a friend or loved one. At Candlemas the 6th house is accented, drawing your attention to animal companions. By February 8 Saturn is retrograde, affecting your finances through the last weeks of winter. Repay old debts; analyze how ongoing patterns, obligations, or legal situations affect your security. From March 6 on, Venus joins Jupiter to trine your Sun. Your 9th house is highlighted. Maintain your faith. Balance will be restored, bringing you peace regarding money matters.

HEALTH

Neptune is completing a 14-year passage through your 6th house of health. Integrate what has been working regarding alternative healing modalities and reject what has not. In early spring, retrograde Mercury makes a quincunx aspect to your Sun. Be aware of how past life or heredity can affect health; you may have to juggle circumstances which seem beyond your control regarding wellness. Once Jupiter enters your sister earth sign of Taurus on June 4 your vitality improves dramatically.

LOVE

With your love sector ruled by serious Saturn, time and patience nurture true love. Give one whom you admire a wrist watch, hourglass, or vintage clock. Pluto affects this part of your horoscope for the next several years, indicating an increasing need for intensity in love relationships. The eclipse of July 1 opposes Pluto, showing that the actions and needs of another can impact the course of romance. August 22 – September 14 and November 27 – December 20 bring favorable transits from Venus and are promising for love.

SPIRITUALITY

Mars, ruler of your 8th house of secrets and the afterlife, makes a long passage through your sign from November 11 through the year's end. It's a perfect time to actively seek new spiritual experiences. The week of the Full Moon in Virgo on March 8, 2012 is especially favorable for deep meditation on your spirituality. Keep a journal handy all year to jot down impressions and make drawings.

FINANCE

Venus rules your 2nd house of money. Explore the hidden symbols in bills and coins; appreciate the history and artistry. Money, both foreign and domestic, has a very magical side. Stack the bills in your wallet with the largest on top, the smallest on the bottom. Fold them toward you and say this traditional money blessing three times: "Divine love through me blesses and increases all that I give and all that I receive. So be it! "

LIBRA
The year ahead for those
born under the sign of the Scales
September 23–October 23

Easygoing, charming, and seeking balance in all things, Libra is the natural diplomat of the zodiac. It's always a challenge to make decisions though. Weighing all the pros and cons of a situation can lead to prevaricating and hedging. Libra is the sign of both war and peace — a reminder that beneath the indecision lurks a steely resolve. Rose quartz, a crystal linked to your ruling planet Venus, is your earth stone.

Love is the theme at the vernal equinox, for Venus and Neptune are both in your 5th house of romance and pleasure. Charge a talisman of rose quartz or pink jade to protect relationships all year. The Full Moon on April 17 is in your sign where it conjoins Saturn. Events unfolding during the four weeks following this significant lunation will be very revealing as to the priorities in your life. Fortunately Saturn, the cosmic taskmaster, is exalted in Libra so the challenges presented can be beneficial in the long run.

From May Eve through early June, Jupiter in Aries is joined by a parade of transits, including Mars and Venus, in your 7th house. Partnerships of all kinds are in a growth phase. New commitments are likely; legal matters can be settled to your satisfaction near the time of the June 1 eclipse. Others make decisions and offer opportunities which impact you. June 3 – 16 brings an exceptional Mercury influence, generating mental clarity and problem-solving ability. Pick a study subject or plan educational travel at this time. As the summer solstice nears, Venus glides into a benevolent aspect to your Sun which lasts until July 4. Pursue summer romances, games, and hobbies.

During the remainder of July strong cardinal sign aspects, channeled toward your career sector, bring distractions and surprises to the workplace. Prepare to multitask and rise to the demands of the moment. At the New Moon in Leo on July 30 and Lammas Eve, Venus and the Sun are in your 11th house. Friends offer helpful suggestions; you can find peace in altruistic activities. The feeling of cooperation and support prevails through early September. On September 15 Venus enters your sign, to be joined by Mercury and the Sun by month's end. An appreciation of fashion, beauty, and culture adds pleasure to the last days of summer and early autumn. Since Saturn is also activated by these transits, structure and values offer comfort to you now. Your birthday brings a sense of accomplishment.

By mid-October you'll feel the impact of a Uranus opposition. Other people are interesting but unpredictable. The Full Moon on October 11 sheds light on the specifics. Be philosophical about eccentric behavior or startling announcements. Detach a bit; focus on yourself and release expectations involving others. From just after Samhain throughout November a strong 3rd house influence prevails. Clear and thoughtful communication assures future success. A neighbor can be more friendly. Be receptive if siblings plan a surprise or have other suggestions regarding the holiday season. The eclipse on November 25 brings the specifics into focus. A reunion can be announced near Thanksgiving. At Yuletide, Venus crosses into your love sector where it remains through January 13. Early winter brings a promise of new love. It's a great time to enjoy the company of children or engage in craft projects.

Just before Candlemas, Mars turns retrograde in your 12th house, where it remains through winter's end. You'll shy away from conflict even more than usual. Release old resentments as you prepare for spring. Winter ends with Neptune, the Sun, and other Pisces transits coming and going in your health sector. Dreams can hold valuable clues to wellness. Sound and color therapies can be very helpful. Pay attention to animal companions; one of them may need some extra TLC by mid-March.

HEALTH

You're very affected by the health and well-being of associates. Steer clear of psychic vampires and drama queens all year. Oppositions from Jupiter and Uranus can soon bring a few your way. Consult a compass school Feng Shui practitioner for ideas about where to place mirrors in order to deflect negative energies from specific areas of concern in the body. If uncertain, the East rules overall health. Position a mirror on the eastern wall of your home or workplace to protect your general well-being.

LOVE

Venus smiles on you during June. Cardinal sign transits move in and out of an unstable T-square aspect this year. Love bonds are in flux; it's not the time to force commitments or promises. The Libra New Moon on September 27 is wonderful for writing a wish list to manifest true love. Mid-September to mid-October and late December to mid-January are promising times to cultivate relationships.

SPIRITUALITY

Pluto is positioned firmly in your sector of housing and family this year and is the focus of several strong aspect patterns, including a square to Saturn, which rules that part of your birth chart. A home meditation area decorated with icons, religious charms, or other spiritual symbols left by family members who have gone before would be helpful.

FINANCE

A Jupiter opposition lasting from the vernal equinox until June 3 warns you to be careful of risky ventures suggested by others. If something sounds too good to be true, back off. Your own instincts are the most trustworthy now. Saturn conjoining the Sun all year indicates the rewards of faithfully following the work ethic and building assets slowly over time. Just after your birthday the results of your efforts begin to bear fruit.

/CORPIV/

SCORPIO
The year ahead for those
born under the sign of the Scorpion
October 24–November 21

Surrounded by an enticing aura of mystery, Scorpio is invariably linked with the word "passionate." Co-ruled by Mars and Pluto, great depth, courage and endurance are present in this sensitive water sign. You're curious about the afterlife and often have an intuitive awareness of subtle energy currents. The bloodstone, long treasured as a healer of wounds, blood purifier, and life extension talisman, is your earth stone.

In early spring, Aquarius transits affect your home and family sector. Redecorating, spring cleaning, or a reunion can be planned before All Fool's Day. During mid-April, Pluto turns retrograde and hovers in your 3rd house until September 17. Keep up with correspondence; allow enough time for commuter travel during this entire time period. You may follow current events more closely than usual. Don't be surprised if you are consulted for an opinion or asked to make a witness statement. In mid-May, Mars enters Taurus, your opposing sign, where it remains until June 20. Challenges and competitive situations present themselves. Although Scorpio rarely compromises, this aspect hints that being a little flexible now might be for the best.

The summer solstice finds Mercury racing to trine your Sun, stirring excitement through the beginning of July. You can learn much through travel and reading. Through late July, Venus reinforces favorable water sign energies. Accept an invitation to go sailing under the Full Moon on the 15th. At Lammastide, celestial lights congregate near your midheaven. Your status and reputation are at a turning point – project the best image possible to important people. You may assume a new position of leadership soon.

August 4 – September 18 Mars moves through your 9th house in a harmonious aspect to your Sun. It's a perfect time to pursue new educational goals or seek spiritual awakening. Your energy level will be high, making it seem easy to complete laborious projects with aplomb. At the autumnal equinox a fixed T-square aspect begins to form, accenting your 1st house through October. There are surprises coming linked to home, partnerships, and/or career issues. Be true to yourself; address one situation at a time. Near the New Moon in your sign on October 26, release stress by gathering an autumn bouquet or visiting an orchard to pick apples. At Samhain, Venus is poised at a conjunction with your Sun. Others are quite loving and supportive. A new fan enters your corner. The Full Moon on November 7 in your relationship sector highlights the specifics of this important connection.

The eclipse pattern in late November to mid-December accents income and investments. New strategies are worth examining. Devote the Yuletide observances to prosperity magic. January finds Jupiter prominent and features various Earth sign transits; partnerships are active. An associate has ideas about business and security needs. Enjoy candlelight during social situations that involve business negotiations. On January 24 Mars begins to retrograde into your 11th house, a trend that lasts through winter's end. Attitudes about long-term goals are changing. Your feelings about several friendships are in flux. Attune to what you really want; if unsure, explore options before finalizing anything. You might mull over unresolved issues with a friend.

On Valentine's Day, Mercury joins Neptune in your 5th house of love. Heed dreams as well as vocal nuances and body language. A deeper bond with one whom you find appealing blossoms by Leap Day. March finds Uranus joined by other transits in your health sector. Prepare healthy, natural meals. Quell the temptation to eat junk food with high calorie or sodium content. Drink plenty of water near the Full Moon on March 8 to flush any impurities from your system.

HEALTH

All year Uranus is poised on the cusp of your 6th house of health, where it reaches out toward a square with Pluto, your ruler. Cardinal signs are involved. There's no time like the present to address health issues. Still, don't be hasty. Be aware of how stress affects health; gather information about options regarding any important health issues. The Full Moon on October 11 can bring the specifics to your attention. With Aries ruling your health, you enjoy trying new and experimental remedies.

LOVE

Neptune is crossing the Pisces cusp, to begin a 14-year passage through your love sector. An idealistic feeling about true love is brewing. Fate, through a set of synchronicities, propels you toward a soulmate by winter's end. Enjoying a romantic movie or theater outing with a loved one can draw you closer together, especially in early April, mid-October, or late February. Surprise the one you care most about with a souvenir album of photos at All Hallows.

SPIRITUALITY

The solar eclipse in Cancer on July 1 highlights your 9th house of the higher mind and spiritual wisdom. It carries truly profound spiritual implications for you. Revere the teachings of various solar and lunar deities, also connect with sacred sea creatures such as dolphins, turtles, and whales. Invoke Sedna, a native Alaskan sea goddess whose name was given to a recently discovered, distant planet. She brings insights into the spirituality of forgiveness.

FINANCE

Four eclipses affect your 2nd and 8th houses of finance this year. It may be necessary to revamp financial plans. Jupiter is in opposition to you from early June through the year's end. It's important to verify claims and credentials impacting finances. A con artist or misinformed financial advisor could be lurking nearby. Call upon an old-time witchcraft from the Deep South to keep this situation in check — eat pecans. They protect and promote prosperity.

SAGITTARIUS
The year ahead for those .
born under the sign of the Archer
November 22–December 21

An optimistic outlook and taking chances just to see how far you can go make the life of a Sagittarian most interesting. This is the sign of the sage, teacher, and religious leader. Animals are an important part of your life. Ruled by Jupiter, largest of planets, you like to consider the big picture. Turquoise is your earth stone. If it's a pure blue-green, it is a wonderful prosperity talisman. When turquoise has black veins it becomes a potent love charm.

As spring begins Mars creates a stir in your home and family life. A relative can be argumentative. Building repairs might be needed. By All Fool's Day, Venus glides in to save the day. Domestic situations steadily improve through late April. A misunderstanding can be harmoniously resolved. Beltane finds Mercury, Venus, Mars, Jupiter, and Uranus clustered in your 5th house of love and pleasure. A captivating new hobby or exciting romantic connection adds zest to the beautiful days of May. The birth of a child or a wedding could be announced near the Full Moon on the 17th.

June brings two eclipses, on the 1st in your 7th house of relationships and on the 15th in your birth sign. Moves are in progress; expect a new career, home, or relationship. Elements of the unpredictable are at work, both within your own psyche and involving others. Release the past and be receptive. From late June through Lammas, Mars challenges you to a showdown as it moves through Gemini, your opposing sign. Associates are stimulating, yet exasperating. Double check legal guidelines and instructions; it's not the time to bend the rules too far. At the same time you can be inspired by high energy, opinionated types. Rest periodically if involved in sports or other forms of physical exertion.

The first three weeks of August Venus joins the Sun in your 9th house of travel. This is lovely for a holiday journey, visit to a spiritual retreat, or enrolling in a seminar. September brings a focus on career goals. A friendly business associate does you a favor before the 14th. At Mabon you'll find deep satisfaction by assisting someone in need. Saturn is accented in your 11th house of humanitarian values. Do-gooder projects absorb your time and attention through All Hallows. On November 3 Mercury and Venus enter your sign. Cultural events, travel, and important discussions highlight the days preceding Yuletide. Eclipses on November 25 and December 10 make this a memorable birthday. Changes which began last June are coming into focus. People enter and leave your life suddenly. At the same time this birthday accents inner growth and new personal interests. Observe the ironic ways you surprise yourself.

On December 25 Jupiter, your ruler, completes its retrograde, and 2012 finds you ready to move forward. During January strong 2nd and 10th house earth sign transits emphasize security. Acquiring extra money, seeking a promotion, and purchasing a long-desired item are priorities. By Candlemas, Mars is retrograde in your career sector. Through the rest of the winter, tone down your natural competitive and assertive traits. It's better to be a bit subtle. Since the health-oriented sign of Virgo is involved, seek ways to make your work environment more wholesome and nurturing.

On February 9 Venus dovetails into a trine with your Sun. A dear one appreciates your kind gestures and responds affectionately during the weeks ahead. A relationship moves into a better place as the winter draws to a close. On Valentine's Day, Mercury enters your home and family sector where it remains until early March. Relatives want to exchange ideas. A store display, publication, or television program can offer marvelous ideas for making your lifestyle better and brighter.

HEALTH

Jupiter, the celestial physician, begins a year-long passage through your health sector on June 4. This year brings a promising time for healing and rising above existing medical problems. Your sign has a way of challenging the body by overindulging in rich food, alcohol, nicotine, etc. Now is the time to overcome any counterproductive health habits or addictions.

LOVE

The Mars-ruled sign of Aries is linked to your love sector, tempting you toward fiery and complex relationships. Complacency bores you. Involvements tend to begin on a high note then fizzle as you lose interest. April – May brings a series of positive influences to your love sector. A romantic getaway to Paris in the springtime would be most delightful. Eclipses zap your 7th house of partnership during June and December. A change of heart is very likely at those times. Important commitments are evolving. Avoid hasty decisions.

SPIRITUALITY

The New Moon on July 30 is a rare Black Moon, the second New Moon in a single month. It falls in your sector of spirituality. A trine to Uranus brings added sparkle. It's a wonderful time to explore fairy magic. A deep meditation beginning at sunset just before Lammas can open the gates to other dimensions. Since Sun-ruled Leo is involved, observe the beautiful colors around sunsets and sunrises to facilitate spiritual awakening.

FINANCE

Pluto will remain in your 2nd house of finances for many years. The changing financial structure of the world is impacting you in a very personal way. Be alert to promising new trends in your professional sphere. Rise to meet challenges. Constructive effort on your part will bring financial rewards during the autumn and winter months. A surprise bonus or other gesture of appreciation is likely to brighten the financial picture near your birthday. Decorate your workspace with deep green and reddish brown hues to enhance prosperity.

CAPRICORN
The year ahead for those
born under the sign of the Goat
December 22–January 19

Trustworthy and reliable, Capricorn has the reputation of being the workaholic of the zodiac. Saturn, the ringed planet, is your ruler, showing a natural respect for boundaries and propriety. Yet, beneath this solemn exterior lurks a wry sense of fun. Jet is your earth stone. Linked especially to Celtic traditions, jet is credited with seven different protective virtues. Enemies, demons, lightning, floods, hunger, getting lost, and accidents are all deflected by this versatile stone.

The vernal equinox accents financial planning. Venus moves to conjoin Neptune in your 2nd house; luck and creativity combine to favorably impact money matters. From early April through late May, Jupiter emphasizes your 4th house. Real estate transactions, relationships with parents, and other decisions concerning home life absorb attention. Conclude purchases and sales of property during this time to assure maximum profits. Saturn completes its retrograde in your career sector during mid-June. By the summer solstice you'll be highly visible at work. Much is demanded of you, but the potential rewards are really great. A Full Moon in your sign

on July 15 brings some important turning points. Your premonitions and dreams are the source of significant wisdom through Lammas.

On August 3 Mars enters your 7th house where it remains until just before Mabon. Other people make plans which include you; be as cooperative as possible. A legal or ethical issue might be open to debate. Visualize a pink bubble surrounding all concerned when discussions grow heated. The New Moon on September 27 through the first week of October brings a tremendous alignment of planets to your 10th house. New career horizons beckon. Your personable demeanor and established reputation impress the right individuals. A promotion or perhaps opening your own business are possible. There is an immediacy to all of this, due to the large number of angular cardinal planets affecting you. Be aware of the preciousness of the current moment. Live fully in and appreciate that most valuable of resources, the present.

By November 3 Mercury and Venus highlight your 12th house. You'll feel the urge to help those less fortunate. You'll also experience a deeper appreciation of ecological concerns and the well-being of wildlife. The eclipse on November 25 brings the specifics into focus. The weeks before your birthday will be happy, for Venus enters your sign on November 26 to remain until the Eve of Yule. Early December is a perfect time to purchase holiday finery and select gifts. Plan a holiday gathering, and accept invitations. There's much to celebrate. The retrograde Mercury pattern during the first half of December can resolve an old puzzle regarding a long-lost friend or relative. It's time to forgive and forget past disappointments.

January begins with a grand trine in Earth signs forming. Your energy level will be high, making it easier to get things done. New Year's week favors research. Consider a business trip or ski holiday January 9 – 27. Just after Candlemas, Neptune exits your financial sector, ending any long-standing nebulousness about security issues. Finally, you will breathe a sigh of relief.

During the last half of February your 3rd house sets the pace. Correspondence, current events, and planning sessions absorb your attention. Expect a great deal of restlessness and multitasking. Near the New Moon on February 21 several interesting short journeys brighten the daily grind. On March 5 Venus enters your love sector, moving toward a conjunction with Jupiter during winter's last days. This is extremely favorable for pursuing love, enjoying children, and art appreciation. Overall, the quality of life is very positive as winter ends.

HEALTH

Your 6th house of health is ruled by talkative Mercury. Discussing health issues, reading about wellness, and participating in healing affirmation circles can be satisfying. During retrograde Mercury cycles be careful not to lapse into any negative health patterns or otherwise neglect your health. The eclipses on June 1 and December 10 directly impact your personal health and the well-being of pets. Be sensitive to new developments linked to wellness.

LOVE

Musically-inclined Taurus watches over your 5th house of love. From the beginning of June through year's end Jupiter covers your love sector with hugs and kisses. You'll be able to choose between new romantic opportunities galore or growing within a single, meaningful relationship. Especially good love cycles include mid-May to early June, late August to mid-September, and the last two weeks of winter.

SPIRITUALITY

You'll actively seek spiritual growth from mid-November through the end of winter as Mars makes a long passage through this sector of your chart. Because pragmatic Virgo is linked to your spiritual growth, you can appreciate the healing elements found in spiritual studies or even the prosperity consciousness of self-help studies. When Mars is retrograde from January 24 through the end of winter, past life regression can be especially rewarding.

FINANCE

Nebulous, elusive Neptune is completing a 14-year passage through your 2nd house of finances. By year's end you'll feel greater clarity regarding the economy and your long-term financial plans than you have in a very long time. Studying the global picture can bring you peace and comfort, especially near the New Moon in Capricorn on December 24. Overall, a supportive pattern of favorable Earth transits should make this a good year for financial growth. This will be especially apparent from the middle of summer through the winter.

AQUARIUS
The year ahead for those
born under the sign of the Water Bearer
January 20–February 18

Uranus, planet of inventions, revolution, and eccentricity, holds the key to understanding this iconoclast of the zodiac. Aquarius is original, amusing, and popular with a genuine charismatic sparkle. A fascination with human nature often brings a focus on psychology and humanitarian ventures. Lapis lazuli is your earth stone. Edgar Cayce recommended that lapis be worn for healing. Mystics credit lapis with added potency when flecks of gold appear in it.

Spring finds Venus in your 1st house. Your charm and good looks open doors and make a good impression. Ask for favors; express affection. During April retrograde Mercury impacts your transportation sector. Allow extra time if traveling, as there could be delays. A vehicle might need repair or replacement by May Eve. During mid-May your sector of residence and relatives is highlighted. The roles of parents and children are changing, reflecting the passing of time. A relative could move in or out of the home. You'll give considerable thought to where and how you really want to live.

By June 3 a lighter mood brews. Mercury, the Sun, and by month's end Venus and Mars are in Gemini, your love and pleasure sector. Network with new acquaintances. Someone may offer an invitation to travel. As the summer solstice approaches, health becomes a focus. Celebrate the new season with a massage, reflexology session, or chakra balancing before July 1. A long passage of Mercury through Leo, your opposing sign, commences with the Independence Day holiday. Others are anxious to keep your attention. Be a very good listener. Valuable ideas can be presented. This especially impacts coordinating daily jobs with fitness programs and getting organized. Enlist help; don't attempt to do everything yourself. Near Lammas a Venus pattern shows that a talented person can be a source of inspiration. The Full Moon in your sign on August 13 sheds light on the roles others play in your life and helps you select associates. As September begins your 8th house is strong. Invested or inherited funds or a financial settlement can materialize by September 9. As Mabon nears, Venus and Saturn are favorable. New friendships can develop if you are traveling, attending classes, or frequenting spiritual meetings. It's a great time to complete creative writing or other assignments. The autumnal equinox ushers in a potent Mars opposition which lasts through November 10. Others respond strongly to you. Avoid confrontational types. Devote the All Hallows ritual to peace and harmony.

Planetary patterns highlight the 11th house during November, and the eclipse in Sagittarius on the 25th underscores this trend. New goals have an appeal; your social circle expands to include new, interesting people. At the winter solstice, Venus enters your sign, bringing a warm and fuzzy influence. Beauty, prosperity, and happiness brighten things through the first half of January. Candlemas arrives with a strong Mercury influence. You'll be talkative and curious. Travel is a perfect way to celebrate your birthday. On February 3 Neptune exits your sign for good. Cobwebs of confusion which have hovered for more than a decade are suddenly brushed away. A more grounded mood prevails. The Full Moon in your 7th house on February 7 brings new insights into others. There is sudden empathy with people you just didn't understand before. During the final weeks of winter a strong 2nd house influence emerges. Financial planning will be a top priority. Perfect a new job skill to enhance your earning ability in March. Cultivation of the self is your theme as winter ends.

HEALTH

The solar eclipse on July 1 falls in your 6th house of health. Heed any wake-up calls your body is sending. Your health is strongly influenced by the Moon. Be aware of how the lunar signs and phases each month correlate with your vitality. Check the Moon's phase at your birth. Each month when that phase returns a time of renewed healing begins. The New Moon on January 23 is in your sign. It's a wonderful time to make a list of written affirmations related to health in honor of your birthday.

LOVE

From July 9 – December 11 Uranus, your ruler, is retrograde in your 3rd house. This can bring a short attention span regarding love; you'll look for a companion who has bright ideas to discuss and who isn't overly intense. A dash of fun and humor attracts you most, and you're changing your mind about many things, love included. You'll attract much admiration near the August 13 Full Moon which makes several strong aspects in your sign. The winter months bring more stability in love.

SPIRITUALITY

All year Saturn affects your spirituality sector. It will be in Libra, its sign of exaltation, making a favorable trine aspect. Air signs are involved. You'll welcome structure, tradition, and tangible beliefs as a source of spiritual support. It's a great time to begin a journal or Book of Shadows and write in it faithfully to create a lasting spiritual tool. Deities related to justice as well as the winds, air, and life breath will be significant to your spiritual journey this year.

FINANCE

Mars makes a long passage through your 8th house this year, from November through the end of winter. This can bring stress with a partner's business decisions or shared expenses. Neptune enters your 2nd house of finances where it will remain for many years. Good or bad, your finances won't be quite as you expect. Dream work can help. As you fall asleep, reflect upon monetary options and opportunities. Within a few nights answers can come.

PISCES

*The year ahead for those
born under the sign of the Fish*
February 19–March 20

You're capable of great sensitivity. This natural empathy with others is so strong that it can be a mixed blessing. Recognize when a situation is having a negative impact. A powerful imagination and appreciation for fantasy and imagery can bring success in spiritual practices and the fine arts. Coral is your earth stone. Wear it to attract love, preserve enjoyment in life, and repel depression.

Spring begins with energy and enthusiasm at a peak, for Mars remains in your sign through All Fool's Day. April 4 – 5 can be important because Neptune, your ruler, first touches the cusp of your sign then, a pattern which hasn't happened in 164 years or so. A premonition of times to come, especially involving your deeper purpose in life, can be revealed. By May Day your financial sector sets the pace. A favorable Jupiter influence is in effect until early June. Add to savings and pursue income-generating opportunities which arise. Wisely managing resources now has a favorable impact on the long-term financial future.

The June 15 lunar eclipse profoundly affects your career situation. Be observant concerning new developments affecting your profession. There can be some excitement afoot. At the summer solstice, Mars creates a stir in your 4th house of family life. The arrival of visitors can be a little unsettling. You'll play peacekeeper for argumentative household members. This trend relaxes once Lammas passes. August finds your health sector highlighted. Since retrograde Mercury is involved, be aware of your health history. Double-check any instructions given by a health care professional. On September 12 the Full Moon in your sign enjoys a favorable Mars aspect, bringing a cycle of accomplishment and enthusiasm your way. At Mabon, bless a tiny silver dolphin or whale charm to wear for luck during autumn.

The last half of October through Samhain, Mercury and Venus move into a benevolent aspect to your Sun. It's an ideal time for a journey. Studies and creative projects are favored too. During November, Mars moves into Virgo, your opposing sign, where it remains through the end of winter. Your 7th house is impacted. This can bring actions on the part of others which will affect you. A close relationship needs attention. Seek ways to turn this potentially competitive trend into an interesting camaraderie. Keep rivalry good-natured, but avoid anyone who is too difficult.

During December, Venus joins Pluto in your 11th house, making a gentle sextile to your Sun. Holiday celebrations, community service, and charitable projects absorb your attention. A new friendship strengthens. There's peace and pleasure in tying up loose ends during the first half of December when Mercury is retrograde. This leaves you free to make plans for the future by Yuletide. Consult the Tarot or another divination tool at the solstice for a meaningful message.

Early January finds Aquarius transits in your 12th house. You'll be rather introspective and prefer to keep a low profile. January 14 – February 8 Venus is in your sign and everything changes. Prepare to bask in a burst of sudden admiration, both among friends and at work. Wear your finest clothes and express creative ideas with eloquence. Romance surrounds you.

The last half of February ushers in a strong aspect pattern in mutable signs. Mercury, Neptune, and Mars are prominent. There can be important meetings or travel. You'll tend to compare yourself to others. Honor your individuality while appreciating what you can learn from associates. Maintain perspective by keeping up with current events, both locally and globally. Old financial issues can need attention in early March – your 2nd house shows some monetary highs and lows. After March 6 positive 3rd house patterns show helpful ideas presenting themselves. The winter concludes on a hopeful note.

HEALTH

Appreciation and positive reinforcement are especially important to your well-being. A kind word will have you literally purring with new energy, as Leo is your 6th house of health indicator. Avoid those who make you feel weak through undermining your confidence. Maintain a sense of humor about health conditions. Explore laughter yoga or slip out to a comedy club. You might be surprised at how healing a good laugh can be.

LOVE

The sign of Cancer rules your love sector. Being familiar with a loved one's past can help you make a decision about the relationship. The July 1 eclipse is square Uranus and in opposition to Pluto. This profoundly affects your love life. A relationship can go in a new direction or even end. Prepare to welcome surprises and new situations directly involving love this year. April, October, and January hold promise for happiness in romance.

SPIRITUALITY

With Scorpio perched on the cusp of your 9th house of spirituality, the mysteries of the afterlife will be a part of your path. The hours between midnight and dawn often play a role in your spiritual awakening, as does dream interpretation. The weeks following the Full Moon in Scorpio on May 17 favor focusing on your spiritual quest. Halloween is another time when the gates of higher awareness are likely to swing open and welcome you inside.

FINANCE

The early weeks of spring find Jupiter blessing your financial sector. Try to finalize decisions and get finances in order before June 4, when Jupiter changes signs. During the rest of the year Uranus, the celestial lightning bolt, holds sway over your 2nd house of money. Prepare for some surprises; you can go from rags to riches and back again. Your interpretation of what constitutes true wealth is in the midst of a catharsis.

Sites of Awe

The Great Trees of the Pacific Northwest

I WAS fortunate enough to be visiting Seattle during a time of the year when I could ask for a tour of the giant trees. A dear friend was kind enough not only to bring me into the thick of things, but also to know that I needed solitude once I got there.

Walking through the tropical forest vicinity, the first thing I noticed was the dampness in the air. Although it was a relatively dry day, as soon as I entered the wooded area I could feel the moisture in the atmosphere. The thickness of the air offered a sign that I would encounter a richness of life that can be found in such places. Everywhere you looked, life sprang from life. Plants were growing out of other living plants. And when a tree fell, it was quickly covered with new life that shortly left it invisible to a passerby. Moss, lichen and fungus abounded. The conifer-dominated forest shone with a green carpet underfoot and a green canopy above.

The environment was both still and busy. Animal, bird and insect life teemed, yet there was a sense of quiet like an outdoor temple. The forest held a majestic feeling of antiquity almost prehistoric in nature, leaving me overwhelmed by wonder. Oddly enough, the massive weight of each tree contributes to its survival. These outsized trees have no taproot and could be blown down easily if they weighed less.

A typical fairy presence reveals itself to the alert by way of hanging dewdrops, faces in the bark, circles of moss, sounds of whispers, isolated breezes and much more. Plants of such age have clouds of fairy activity about them – clusters of nature spirits tending to the forest and its creatures.

Care to take a piece of antiquity home? Bring an offering of water for the tree and bread for the earth spirits. Leave the offerings in the forest and choose a charm for yourself – a fallen branch, pine cone, a stone, pine needles or a fallen leaf. With your offering, ask a boon of the oldest living things on earth.

– ARMAND TABER

Spirit Rock

Prophesy of the sacred Earth stone

AMONG Native American earth stone traditions, the legend of Spirit Rock is unique and poignant, a mystery in granite. Located on Highway 55 in Northern Wisconsin, near the towns of Keshena, Shawno and Antigo, Spirit Rock is surrounded by a protective log fence always freshly painted white. A roadside historical marker tells the story.

Spirit Rock contains the record of the local Menominee Indians provided by a dream that came to Manabush, a founder of the Medicine Society. Manabush was a powerful shaman, a medicine man. The dream foretold that eventually Spirit Rock would crumble away with age until it completely disappeared. When this happened, the Menominee tribe would die out. This story has been recorded by archaeologists since at least 1914, when the rock was almost a boulder. It was loaf shaped, about five feet high and five feet long. The rock rests on the St. Croix Trail, a major thoroughfare used by woodland Indians, and visitors noticed that sacred offerings of tobacco, herbs and other gifts were always left near this site. The Native Americans passed by in silent reverence. Eventually they shared the story.

Future of forecast?

The old St. Croix Trail became the main highway through the Menominee Reservation, an area set aside for the Indians in an 1854 treaty. The highway builders left Spirit Rock intact and admiring visitors can still gaze from outside the protective log fence. The rock commands a quiet respect. The offerings to placate the Great Spirit continue to appear through the years. But by the late 1960s, Spirit Rock had dwindled to about three feet long and two feet high. A recent photo shows that the sacred rock is now nearly invisible. It's pancake flat, a slab, barely above the ground. If there is truth in the prophecy, the days of this small woodland tribe are indeed numbered.

Perhaps there is a link with the coming earth changes of 2012. The time is close by. Many indigenous peoples and soothsayers throughout the ages feel that 2012 marks the end of one phase of life on Earth. Presently the Menominee seem to be doing well. But during most of the twentieth century, the tribe was desperately poverty stricken, ill with tuberculosis, ravaged by alcoholism and measles. Now casinos have brought the tribe great wealth. A college and hospital built on the reservation have improved the quality of life and life expectancy. Only in time will the genuine importance of Spirit Rock and the truth (or lack thereof) of its unique story be revealed. Meanwhile this sacred earth stone offers a wonderful site of easy pilgrimage to seekers who would reflect upon the old ways.

– Dikki Jo Mullen

Reviews

Traditional Witchcraft:
A Cornish Book of Ways
by Gemma Gary.
Troy Books (Oct 2008)
www.troybooks.co.uk
ISBN 978-0956104304

IT SEEMS that witches and cunning folk have been a part of the Cornish landscape for as long as there has been a Cornwall. Long forgotten folkloric customs remain prominent in some Cornish towns while colorful celebrations of seasonal holidays draw crowds of locals and visitors alike. Gemma Gary presents a fascinating look into unique Cornish witchcraft beliefs and the West Country ways of local witches, charmers, conjurors, and pellars. Gary's book is a syncretic mixture of older traditional practices and modern innovations by the author and her close associates. This book will expand your vocabulary of terms and enhance your understanding of how witchcraft can still find a place in a modern day social marketplace.

In the Dark Places of Wisdom
by Peter Kingsley
The Golden Sufi Center
(December 1, 1999)
ISBN 978-1890350017

DR. PETER Kingsley is not content to simply rehash academic philosophical canon. Instead he weaves a new vision of the ancient world and presents a compelling case for how we got from there to here. While books about classical philosophy are often sterile and dry, this book is a fertile field of epiphanic discovery, ripe with ideas still fresh despite the passing of ages.

In the Dark Places of Wisdom is about the pre-Socratic philosopher Parmenides, also a practicing priest of Apollo and healer. He wrote about a descent to the Underworld, and the practice of "incubation" as a means to gain wisdom and understanding through connection to divine consciousness. Packed with insight and backed up by solid scholarship *In the Dark Places of Wisdom* is written for the inquisitive mind and does not disappoint.

Tales from the Crow Man
by Damh The Bard

DAMH (pronounced Dave), a modern-day bard, is a frequent performer at pagan events in the UK. In keeping with the bardic tradition, he draws inspiration for his music from the realms of myth and mystery. Damh has produced four CD's of original songs. *Tales from the Crow Man*, his fifth CD, contains modern interpretations of classic folk songs. My personal favorite is Damh's haunting version of *The Green*

Fields of France, a powerful anti-war song. These songs are time honored tunes which inspire and enchant. If you welcome this CD into your home it is sure to quicken your step and warm your heart. Available to US customers from CDBaby and iTunes. Links are available on his website: http://www.paganmusic.co.uk/

Alice In Wonderland (2010)

DESPITE spectacular art direction and an all star cast, Tim Burton's film adaptation of Lewis Carroll's classic novels, *Alice's Adventures in Wonderland* and *Through the Looking-Glass*, has not garnered many rave reviews from the mainstream media. However the combination of live action with animation is successfully accomplished making the fantastic elements come alive in a believable and enjoyable way. The story line involves a now nineteen year old Alice accidentally returning to Underland, a place she had visited in dreams years before and misheard as Wonderland. Perhaps the departure from Lewis Carroll's original work was a bridge too far for some, but this reviewer welcomes the subtle transformation of Wonderland into a version of Elphame. The familiar characters who inhabit Underworld are transformed into comfortable adult presentations.

Available on Blue Ray and DVD.

TO: The Witches' Almanac, P.O. Box 1292, Newport, RI 02840-9998
www.TheWitchesAlmanac.com

Name_____

Address_____

City_____ State_____ Zip_____

E-mail_____

WITCHCRAFT being by nature one of the secretive arts, it may not be as easy to find us next year. If you'd like to make sure we know where you are, why don't you send us your name and address? You will certainly hear from us.

From a Witch's Mailbox

Food for Thought

We will be starting our garden soon and were wondering if there are any herbs we can grow to aid our practice?

Jessica and Jamie E.
Holyoke, MA

Many kitchen herbs are grown for their magical as well as culinary uses. For example, basil is commonly used in love potions, rosemary to ward off nightmares, and dill to ease nervous afflictions. Keep your garden stocked with a variety of herbs and you will never be lacking for ingredients, be it in your spells or your cooking.

A Familiar Question

How can I keep my familiar strong and happy?

– Jim S.
Rutgers, VT

In the preface to the last Almanac, we said, "Appreciate your familiars for what they are – a loving extension of ourselves." In this sense, the best way to take care of your familiar is to take care of yourself. Eat healthy, exercise, and take time each day to relax or else your stress will inevitably become your familiar's. In addition, you can feed them energy-charged water. Set a dish in the sun or moonlight and meditate

on your intentions for your familiar: healthfulness, longevity or anything else you may wish for your furry friend (or feathery, or scaly…).

Love is in the Air

Can you please recommend a simple, discreet love spell that doesn't require a whole bunch of special ingredients?

– Lonely in Liverpool
e-mail

Those of you who live in the Northern Hemisphere are in luck. This spell calls upon the celestial powers of the Ursa Major, Ursa Minor and Draco constellations. Locate these stars in the night sky and gazing upon them, recite this old Irish wishing charm:

> Great bear, small bear,
> In the serpent winding;
> Hear now a simple prayer
> That love I may be finding.

(from Magic Spells and Incantations *by Elizabeth Pepper)*

Someone's in the Kitchen with Chloe

Are you planning to release any new cooking videos? Chloe's Rosemary Shortbread recipe was an absolute hit at our last Beltane!

– Clair C.
Burbank, CA

Look for a new Witches' Pantry video on our website in the coming months. This time Chloe is cooking up something spectacular (think LOTS of Garlic!).

Magical Distinctions

I just saw the Aleister Crowley movie. Was he a witch?

– Sarah Q.
e-mail

No, Crowley was a magician. Although Crowley knew and socialized with witches, he never professed to be one. While witches work with *spiritual or natural forces, a magician achieves his aims through the imposition of his will* upon *those forces. A witch asks the rabbit to come out of the hat; a magician tells it to.*

The Almanac Anywhere

I live in a small town and have trouble finding a physical copy of the Almanac. Any suggestions?

– Eric L.
e-mail

Visit www.TheWitchesAlmanac.com to order current and back issues of the almanac direct from us. Or, ask your favorite local bookstore to carry us! They can order by contacting Sales@ TheWitchesAlmanac.com.

Yule Tidings

Got any ideas for inexpensive Yule gifts? We are on a budget but still want to give our covenmates something special.

– Salvatore M.
e-mail

Sometimes the best gifts are the simplest, and nothing is more special than a handmade gift. Make a rune set out of smooth beach stones, bundle dry herbs grown from your own garden, or charge a pair of candles with intentions for prosperity in the coming year. Better yet, write each of your covenmates a personalized poem to let them know how important they are to you.

Let us hear from you, too

We love to hear from our readers. Letters should be sent with the writer's name (or just first name or initials), address, daytime phone number and e-mail address, if available. Published material may be edited for clarity or length. All letters and e-mails will become the property of The Witches' Almanac Ltd. and will not be returned. We regret that due to the volume of correspondence we cannot reply to all communications.

The Witches' Almanac, Ltd.
P.O. Box 1292
Newport, RI 02840-9998
info@TheWitchesAlmanac.com
www.TheWitchesAlmanac.com

The products and services offered above are paid advertisements.

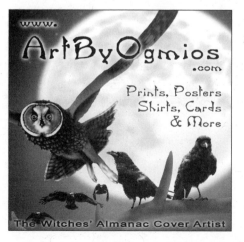
The products and services offered above are paid advertisements.

The products and services offered above are paid advertisements.

The HORNED SHEPHERD
by EDGAR JEPSON

Woodcuts by WILFRED JONES

WANDER THE MAGICAL WORLD of the Valley of Fine Fleeces with a fascinating cast of characters. Meet Big Anna, keeper of both the pagan flame and Cross; a Princess aflame for a strange lover; an Egyptian Priest, steward of mysteries; Friar Paul, lean and sinister; and Saccabe the Black Goat, Father of Many Flocks. Above all you will encounter the mysterious Shepherd of supernatural radiance, among whose curls nestle two small soft horns. Events converge in the forest on Midsummer Eve at full moon as celebrants arrive with meat, bread and wine for the Feast. The Wise Ones recognize the Horned Shepherd as an ancient fertility god who should be sacrificed to enrich the land. Beautiful woodcuts enhance the 146-page book. $16.95

ঌ *Newly expanded classics!* ঌ

The ABC of Magic Charms
Elizabeth Pepper

SINCE THE DAWN of mankind, an obscure instinct in the human spirit has sought protection from mysterious forces beyond mortal control. Human beings sought benefaction in the three realms that share Earth with us — animal, mineral, vegetable. All three, humanity discovered, contain mysterious properties discovered over millennia through occult divination. An enlarged edition of *Magic Charms from A to Z*, compiled by the staff of *The Witches' Almanac.* $12.95

The Little Book of Magical Creatures
Elizabeth Pepper and Barbara Stacy
A loving tribute to the animal kingdom

AN UPDATE of the classic *Magical Creatures*, featuring Animals Tame, Animals Wild, Animals Fabulous – plus an added section of enchanting animal myths from other times, other places. *A must for all animal lovers.* $12.95

♣ a lady shape-shifts into a white doe
♣ two bears soar skyward
♣ Brian Boru rides a wild horse
♣ a wolf growls dire prophecy

ARADIA
GOSPEL OF THE WITCHES
Charles Godfrey Leland

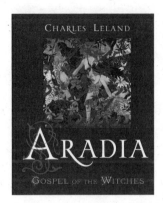

ARADIA IS THE FIRST work in English in which witchcraft is portrayed as an underground old religion, surviving in secret from ancient pagan times.

• Used as a core text by many modern neo-pagans.

• Foundation material containing traditional witchcraft practices

• This special edition features appreciations by such authors and luminaries as Paul Huson, Raven Grimassi, Judika Illes, Michael Howard, Christopher Penczak, Myth Woodling, Christina Oakley Harrington, Patricia Della-Piana, Jimahl di Fiosa and Donald Weiser. A beautiful and compelling work, this edition has brought the format up to date, while keeping the text unchanged. 172 pages $16.95

The Witchcraft of Dame Darrel of York
Charles Godfrey Leland

Introduction by Robert Mathiesen

 NEVER before published, this beautifully reproduced clothbound facsimile of the illuminated manuscript includes a full transcript of the text. A possible model for the first modern Book of Shadows, this hand illuminated manuscript is evidence of Leland's years of brilliant research. Not entirely fiction, and a product of Leland's imaginative genius, *The Witchcraft of Dame Darrel of York* purports to be the full account of the witchcraft practiced in medieval England. A composition of this type leaves room for readers to create their own practice rooted in tradition, yet responsive to twentieth century needs. Hardcover. 400 pages.

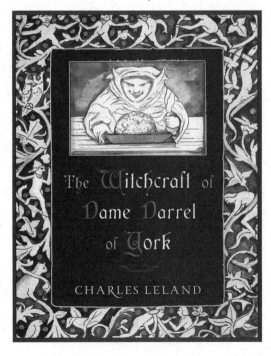

Witches All

A Treasury from past editions...

Perfect for study or casual reading, Witches All *is a collection from* The Witches' Almanac *publications of the past. Arranged by topics, the book, like the popular almanacs, is thought provoking and often spurs me on to a tangent leading to even greater discovery. The information and art in the book – astrological attributes, spells, recipes, history, facts & figures is a great reminder of the history of the Craft, not just in recent years, but in the early days of the Witchcraft Revival in this century: the witch in an historical and cultural perspective.* Ty Bevington, Circle of the Wicker Man, Columbus, Ohio

Absolutely beautiful! I recently ordered Witches All *and I have to say I wasn't disappointed. The artwork and articles are first rate and for a longtime* Witches' Almanac *fan, it is a wonderful addition to my collection.* Witches' Almanac *devotees and newbies alike will love this latest effort. Very worth getting.*
Tarot3, Willits, California

GREEK GODS IN LOVE

Barbara Stacy casts a marvelously original eye on the beloved stories of Greek deities, replete with amorous oddities and escapades. We relish these tales in all their splendor and antic humor, and offer an inspired storyteller's fresh version of the old, old mythical magic.

MAGIC CHARMS FROM A TO Z

A treasury of amulets, talismans, fetishes and other lucky objects compiled by the staff of *The Witches' Almanac*. An invaluable guide for all who respond to the call of mystery and enchantment.

LOVE CHARMS

Love has many forms, many aspects. Ceremonies performed in witchcraft celebrate the joy and the blessings of love. Here is a collection of love charms to use now and ever after.

MAGICAL CREATURES

Mystic tradition grants pride of place to many members of the animal kingdom. Some share our life. Others live wild and free. Still others never lived at all, springing instead from the remarkable power of human imagination.

ANCIENT ROMAN HOLIDAYS

The glory that was Rome awaits you in Barbara Stacy's classic presentation of a festive year in pagan times. Here are the gods and goddesses as the Romans conceived them, accompanied by the annual rites performed in their worship. Scholarly, light-hearted – a rare combination.

CELTIC TREE MAGIC

Robert Graves in *The White Goddess* writes of the significance of trees in the old Celtic lore. *Celtic Tree Magic* is an investigation of the sacred trees in the remarkable Beth-Luis-Nion alphabet; their role in folklore, poetry, and mysticism.

MOON LORE

As both the largest and the brightest object in the night sky, and the only one to appear in phases, the Moon has been a rich source of myth for as long as there have been mythmakers.

MAGIC SPELLS
AND INCANTATIONS

Words have magic power. Their sound, spoken or sung, has ever been a part of mystic ritual. From ancient Egypt to the present, those who practice the art of enchantment have drawn inspiration from a treasury of thoughts and themes passed down through the ages.

LOVE FEASTS

Creating meals to share with the one you love can be a sacred ceremony in itself. With the witch in mind, culinary adept Christine Fox offers magical menus and recipes for every month in the year.

RANDOM RECOLLECTIONS
I, II, III, IV

Pages culled from the original (no longer available) issues of *The Witches' Almanac*, published annually throughout the 1970's, are now available in a series of tasteful booklets. A treasure for those who missed us the first time around; keepsakes for those who remember.

Order form on back page

News from The Witches' Almanac

Glad tidings from the staff

The Witches' Almanac is 40 years old!

Our publication began in 1971 and this year we are celebrating our 40th birthday! We would like to express heartfelt thanks to Elizabeth Pepper, Barbara Stacy and all the dedicated writers, editors, artists and other folks that have contributed to making this possible throughout the years.

Two new publications

A remarkable discovery, *The Witchcraft of Dame Darrel of York*, is a handwritten, illustrated manuscript penned by Charles Godfrey Leland. Perhaps the first modern Book of Shadows, this original work has never been published. Scholars, collectors and enthusiasts alike will delight in our beautifully reproduced clothbound facsimile of the original manuscript which incudes a full transcription of the text. Explore the creative genius of Leland portrayed through his writing and extensive original artwork. Available in a standard, special boxed or leather edition.

Originally published in 1899, *Aradia: Gospel of the Witches*, is likely the most celebrated source text of the modern witchcraft revival. The Witches' Almanac, Ltd. brings you a special edition of Charles Godfrey Leland's classic work. Readers will recognize our trademark quality complete with classic illustrations, impeccable typography and faithful preservation of the original text. Serious students of the occult will appreciate the introduction by Professor Robert Matthiesen and commentary by notable authors such as Paul Huson, Raven Grimassi and Michael Howard. This editon is a must-have for every discriminating collector.

UK Distribution

The Witches' Almanac is now being sold in the United Kingdom. Look for your favorite titles in the shops of London, Glastonbury and other suppliers of fine occult books.

Going Green

In our ongoing effort to help Mother Earth, *The Witches' Almanac* is once again printed on recycled paper! Help our campaign – sign up for our email newsletter at http://TheWitchesAlmanac.com/emailform.html.

Order Form

Each timeless edition of *The Witches' Almanac* is unique.
Limited numbers of previous years' editions are available.

Item	Price	Qty.	Total
2011-2012 The Witches' Almanac	$11.95		
2010-2011 The Witches' Almanac	$11.95		
2009-2010 The Witches' Almanac	$11.95		
2008-2009 The Witches' Almanac	$10.95		
2007-2008 The Witches' Almanac	$9.95		
2006-2007 The Witches' Almanac	$8.95		
2005-2006 The Witches' Almanac	$8.95		
2004-2005 The Witches' Almanac	$8.95		
2003-2004 The Witches' Almanac	$8.95		
2002-2003 The Witches' Almanac	$7.95		
2001-2002 The Witches' Almanac	$7.95		
2000-2001 The Witches' Almanac	$7.95		
1999-2000 The Witches' Almanac	$7.95		
1998-1999 The Witches' Almanac	$6.95		
1997-1998 The Witches' Almanac	$6.95		
1996-1997 The Witches' Almanac	$6.95		
1995-1996 The Witches' Almanac	$6.95		
1994-1995 The Witches' Almanac	$5.95		
1993-1994 The Witches' Almanac	$5.95		
The Witchcraft of Dame Darrel of York, clothbound	$65.00		
Aradia or The Gospel of the Witches	$16.95		
The Horned Shepherd	$16.95		
The ABC of Magic Charms	$12.95		
The Little Book of Magical Creatures	$12.95		
Greek Gods in Love	$15.95		
Witches' All	$13.95		
Ancient Roman Holidays	$6.95		
Celtic Tree Magic	$7.95		
Love Charms	$6.95		
Love Feasts	$6.95		
Magic Charms from A to Z	$12.95		
Magical Creatures	$12.95		
Magic Spells and Incantations	$12.95		
Moon Lore	$7.95		
Random Recollections II	$3.95		
Random Recollections III	$3.95		
Random Recollections IV	$3.95		
Bundle of 13 back issues *(with free book bag)*	$75.00		
The Rede of the Wiccae	$22.95		
Keepers of the Flame	$20.95		
Subtotal			
Tax (7% sales tax for RI customers)			
Shipping & Handling *(See shipping rates section)*			
TOTAL			

BRACELETS			
Item	**Price**	**Qty.**	**Total**
Agate, Green	$5.95		
Agate, Moss	$5.95		
Agate, Natural	$5.95		
Agate, Red	$5.95		
Amethyst	$5.95		
Aventurine	$5.95		
Fluorite	$5.95		
Jade, African	$5.95		
Jade, White	$5.95		
Jasper, Picture	$5.95		
Jasper, Red	$5.95		
Lapis Lazuli	$5.95		
Malachite	$5.95		
Moonstone	$5.95		
Obsidian	$5.95		
Onyx, Black	$5.95		
Opal	$5.95		
Quartz Crystal	$5.95		
Quartz, Rose	$5.95		
Rhodonite	$5.95		
Sodalite	$5.95		
Tigereye	$5.95		
Turquoise	$5.95		
Unakite	$5.95		
Subtotal			
Tax (7% for RI customers)			
Shipping & Handling (*See shipping rates section*)			
TOTAL			

MISCELLANY			
Item	**Price**	**Qty.**	**Total**
Pouch	$3.95		
Matches: *10 small individual boxes*	$5.00		
Matches: *1 large box of 50 individual boxes*	$20.00		
Natural/Black Book Bag	$17.95		
Red/Black Book Bag	$17.95		
Hooded Sweatshirt, Blk	$30.00		
Hooded Sweatshirt, Red	$30.00		
L-Sleeve T, Black	$20.00		
L-Sleeve T, Red	$20.00		
S-Sleeve T, Black/W	$15.00		
S-Sleeve T, Black/R	$15.00		
S-Sleeve T, Dk H/R	$15.00		
S-Sleeve T, Dk H/W	$15.00		
S-Sleeve T, Red/B	$15.00		
S-Sleeve T, Ash/R	$15.00		
S-Sleeve T, Purple/W	$15.00		
Postcards – set of 12	$3.00		
Bookmarks – set of 12	$1.00		
Magnets – set of 3	$1.50		
Promo Pack	$7.00		
Subtotal			
Tax (7% sales tax for RI customers)			
Shipping & Handling (*See shipping rates section*)			
TOTAL			

SHIPPING & HANDLING CHARGES

BOOKS: One book, add $4.00. Each additional book add $1.50

POUCH: One pouch, $2.00. Each additional pouch add $1.50

MATCHES: Ten individual boxes, add $2.50.
One large box of fifty, add $6.00. Each additional large box add $3.50.

BOOKBAGS: $4.00 per bookbag.

BRACELETS: $2.00 per bracelet.

Send a check or money order payable in U. S. funds or credit card details to:

The Witches' Almanac, Ltd., PO Box 1292, Newport, RI 02840-9998

(401) 847-3388 (phone) • (888) 897-3388 (fax)
Email: info@TheWitchesAlmanac.com • www.TheWitchesAlmanac.com